DATE			

Apocalyptic Messianism and Contemporary
Jewish-American Poetry

SUNY Series in Modern Jewish Literature and Culture
Sarah Blacher Cohen, Editor

Apocalyptic Messianism and Contemporary Jewish-American Poetry

R. Barbara Gitenstein

State University of New York Press

Published by
State University of New York Press, Albany
For information, address State University of New York
Press, State University Plaza, Albany, N.Y., 12246

Library of Congress Cataloging-in-Publication Data

Gitenstein, R. Barbara, 1948-
 Apocalyptic messianism and contemporary
Jewish-American poetry.

 (SUNY series in modern Jewish literature
and culture)
 Bibliography: p. 125
 Includes index.
 1. American poetry—Jewish authors—History
and criticism. 2. Jewish religious poetry,
American—History and criticism. 3. Apocalyptic
literature—History and criticism. 4. Messiah
in literature. 5. American poetry—20th century—
History and criticism. I. Title. II. Series.

PS153.J4G5 1985   811'.54'098924   85—12542
ISBN 0-88706-154-0
ISBN 0-88706-155-9 (pbk.)

For my Mother, Shekinah in Exile

Contents

Preface

*A*pocalyptic *Messianism and Contemporary Jewish-American Poetry* is an analysis of how an overlooked Jewish tradition has influenced an overlooked literary genre: apocalyptic messianism is overlooked by rabbinic authority and Jewish-American poetry by literary critics. I have chosen to discuss the apocalyptic messianic influence for two reasons: first, its influence is growing, both in the number and significance of the poets manifesting this influence, and in the variety of apocalyptic references that make up that influence; and second, it is a surprising influence, contradictory to the rabbinic interpretation of Judaism.

Though the body of Jewish-American poetry is more various than the analysis might imply, the limitation of the study provides some revealing conclusions about the literary canon of American Jews, particularly in contrast with that of European Jews. As is made clear in my first chapter on definitions, a tie is indicated between a group of contemporary poets and one esoteric aspect of the long heritage of *kabbalah*. The series of books necessary to discuss the *kabbalistic* influence on twentieth-century Jewish-American poetry will be long and complex, with at least one volume dedicated to the study of the *Zohar's* impact. But the restricted focus is a limitation in types of sources, not types of poetry. The poetry discussed is remarkably various, ranging from John Hollander's formalistic verse, to Jerome Rothenberg's open-ended forms.

A quick survey of critical essays or books on Jewish-American literature reveals precious little discussion of poetry. In fact, one might come to suspect from such an overview that there is no poetry written by Jews in America. Such is not the case, as evidenced by the numerous individual publications which are cited in the accompanying bibliography, as well as by several recent anthologies, most particularly Jerome Rothenberg's *A Big Jewish Book* and Howard Schwartz's *Voices Within the Ark*. Neither of these collections is strictly American, but Schwartz's collection of world poets includes poetry by over one hundred Americans writing in English, and Rothenberg's text supplements that collection. The introduction will provide the reader with a short historical framework for this poetry, a framework within which to place the poets chosen for discussion. The poetic variety of the artists, their individual importance in movements seminal to contemporary poetry, and the excellence of particular poems form the argument for their inclusion in this analysis.

This book consists of an introduction, four chapters, and a conclusion. The introduction, as described, argues for the value of Jewish-American poetry in general and the poets analyzed in this study, in particular. Chapter 1 defines terms and describes an historical context for understanding these terms. The next three chapters follow a pattern suggested by *kabbalistic* exegesis, each chapter indicating a greater abstraction in symbolic level: literal, allegorical or symbolic, and mystical. Chapter 2 provides some theoretical discussion of apocalyptic historiography and an analysis of poems and novels about individual messianic aspirants and the character of the Messiah in general. The novels are essentially historical fiction, the poems, narrative and descriptive. Chapter 3 provides an analysis of poems that depend on the allegorical patterns of Hebrew angelology, the mirror images of *Shekinah*/Lilith, the spiritual beings who traditionally follow historical messianic hopefuls, the Lurianic myth of creation, and the apocalyptic interpretation of historical epic. These moralistic poems center their thematic concerns on the fearfulness of antinomianism and man's constant struggle to communicate with God. Chapter 4 provides analyses of poems in which the artist articulates mystical answers to ontological questions. These poets find symbolic structure in *kabbalistic* emanation theory and interpretation of the Hebrew alphabet. The conclusion argues for the significance of the appearance of this particular temperament in contemporary literature.

Acknowledgments

I owe a debt of gratitude to a great number of people and several institutions. I would like to thank the staff and administration of the Ward Edwards Library of Central Missouri State University where I conducted most of my research. Everyone there was helpful, but a few names must be singled out: Patricia Downing sought out copies of the most esoteric of texts with patience and good humor; Linda Medaris answered innummerable questions related to the research; and Bonnie MacEwan gave me the professional expertise of her speciality as well as that extra encouragement that comes from a good friend. I also wish to thank several colleagues from the English and the Modern Languages Departments at Central Missouri State University for help in various aspects of my research: G. B. Crump, Thomas Gladsky, Mark Johnson, and Susan Pentlin. Without the support of the chairman of the English Department, Larry Olpin, and the Dean of the College of Arts and Sciences, Joseph T. Hatfield, I would never have had the time to finish this manuscript.

Central Missouri State University granted me a paid leave of absence for the year 1981 to 1982, during which time I conducted the bulk of the research for this project. There are many libraries that supported the research through CMSU's interlibrary loan program; the Jewish Collection of the New York Public Library and the

YIVO Library in New York were the two research libraries at which I conducted the basic research.

And finally, I wish to thank my husband Don and my daughter Pauline who supported and encouraged me in this as in all other projects and aspects of my life.

The following publishers have generously given permission to use quotations from copyrighted works:

"For T.S.E. Only." Copyright © 1959 by Hyam Plutzik. Reprinted from *Apples From Shinar*, by permission of Wesleyan University Press.

"The Prophet Announces" and "A Short History." Copyright © 1966 by Harvey Shapiro. Reprinted from *Battle Report* by permission of Wesleyan University Press.

Jerome Rothenberg, *Poland: 1931.* Copyright © by Jerome Rothenberg. Reprinted by permission of New Directions Publishing Corp.

Jerome Rothenberg, *Vienna Blood.* Copyright © 1980 by Jerome Rothenberg. Reprinted by permission of New Directions Publishing Corp.

Gershom G. Scholem, *Major Trends in Jewish Mysticism.* Copyright © 1941 by Schocken Publishing House, Jerusalem. Reprinted by permission of Schocken Books Inc., New York.

Gershom Scholem, *The Messianic Idea in Judaism.* Copyright © 1971 by Schocken Books Inc., New York. Reprinted by permission.

The False Messiah by Leonard Wolf. Copyright © 1982 by Leonard Wolf. Reprinted by permission of Houghton Mifflin Company.

Introduction

A quirk of Jewish-American literary criticism is that it is almost exclusively about prose fiction. Since poetry is a major genre in all Jewish diaspora literatures and since Jewish-American literature has a history of approximately one hundred years, the absence of poets in the tradition would at least be worth noting. But the absence has rarely been noted, much less discussed, in studies of Jewish-American literature. Harold Bloom, in the forefront here as elsewhere, acknowledges the possibility of such a genre when he writes "though it causes me real grief to say this, the achievement of American-Jewish poets down to the present moment remains a modest and mixed one."[1] But Bloom speculates on future achievements. He sees promise in some of the poets writing in 1976, including Irving Feldman and John Hollander, and he predicts the quality that will characterize mature Jewish-American poetry: a combination of devotional intent and romantic vision.[2] Bloom's sympathy for Jewish-American poetry, reiterated in his evaluations of Hollander's *Spectral Emanations*, is an anticipatory one: the poetry shows some promise, but only at some future point will it become a worthy genre. The accuracy of Bloom's analysis of the poetry is limited only by his implication that Jewish-American poetry is without a history. He does not see that this poetry did not spring full grown from the heads of such contemporaries as Jerome

Rothenberg, David Meltzer, Irving Feldman, or John Hollander. Earlier poets, like Emma Lazarus and Charles Reznikoff, get short shrift from Bloom. The poetry discussed in this study, influenced by esoteric sources from subterranean cultures, must be understood as a subsection of the third, and most recent, era in the history of Jewish-American poetry.

The first period of Jewish-American poetry includes mostly lyrics by nineteenth-century precursors of such secular Jewish-American gurus as Saul Bellow and Bernard Mulamud. These poets wrote as much for the Gentile audience as for the Jewish. Their forms showed significant debts to western literary traditions and their diction and rhetoric either aped their Christian counterparts or assumed the mask of Culture Jew. Even their ideas of Jew owed much to the Christians' definition of Jew. Emma Lazarus and Penina Moise are representative of this period.[3] Interestingly enough, these two poets derive not from the Ashkenazic but from the Sephardic past. Therefore, they are in no way tied to the Yiddish culture or the East European sensibility that was to be such a significant factor in the Jewish-American literature of the twentieth century, particularly the fiction. The Sephardim have been established in the United States for almost two centuries, whereas the German Jews immigrated primarily in the middle of the nineteenth century. Since the Sephardic assimilation was apparent even in the mid-nineteenth century,[4] these poets are quite predictably knowledgeable of the English literary verse popular in America during their lifetimes.

Penina Moise lived all her life in Charleston, South Carolina, where she belonged to the old Sephardic community. Though her life was hard after her father's death, she avoided bitterness by dedicating her life to the service of the Jewish community. Some of that service was her poetry. In 1833, she published *Fancy's Sketchbook*, a collection of original verse, which was religious and quite traditional. Her hymns, for which she is still remembered, are included in the Reform Jewish *Union Hymnal*. One of her best known, "Into the Tomb of Ages Past," a Rosh Hashanah hymn, often sung to a traditional "Adon Olam" melody, is written in iambic tetrameter; each of the stanzas includes three masculine rhymed couplets.[5] The topics of the mutability of human life, the speed of time's passage, the dedication to God's laws, and the prayer for peace are all typical of and appropriate to the New Year season. The language is the elevated rhetoric of the nineteenth-century religious poets, both Jewish and Christian. In fact, except for the melody, which is distinctively Jewish, and the absence of the name Jesus Christ, this hymn might have appeared in any Protestant hymnal of the 1830s.

Emma Lazarus' earliest poetry shows no Jewish influence, but her *Songs of a Semite* (1882) has been called the birth volume of Jewish-American poetry. Her most famous poem, the sonnet "The New Colossus" (1883), describes the new Statue of Liberty and the new country as "Mother of Exiles," resting place for all who suffer rejection in the ancient European cultures.[6] Though no immigrant could be pleased to be called any country's "wretched refuse," America's open arms must have seemed more pleasant to the immigrants than the pogroms of Eastern Europe. Lazarus, not an immigrant, but a member of America's Sephardic elite, would not have seen this image as offensive, but rather as generous.

Emma Lazarus published her first volume of poetry in 1866. *Admetus and Other Poems*, (1871) manifests a great debt to traditional western culture but has no reference to Judaism. Only after George Eliot's 1876 *Daniel Deronda* did Lazarus become a Jewish poet. Her study of medieval Sephardic poets and of Heinrich Heine joined with her American literary study to result in her "New Colossus," a personal version of the self-serving nineteenth-century American image of ourselves. In the 1880s, Lazarus's poetry was praised by such famous Americans as William Cullen Bryant, John Greenleaf Whittier, Ralph Waldo Emerson, and Walt Whitman. "The New Colossus," an Italian sonnet, begins with the contrast between the American monuments to culture and the classic European monuments. Symbolized by a powerful female whose torch lights the way to new world freedom, the "Mother of Exiles" tells the ancient world to send the "tired," the "poor," and the "huddled masses" to America. This sonnet, significant as an expression of late nineteenth-century America's self-image, marks the character of the first era of Jewish-American poetry. Its melting pot theory, so precious to the majority in American culture, as expressed by someone inspired to admit her Jewishness by a Christian novel, was a most appropriate inscription for that French gift, Miss Liberty, that stands in the New York harbor. The early poetry is highly conventional and only belatedly Jewish.

The poets of the second major historical era, the Modernists and Experimentalists, were quite scholarly and intellectual, and, for the most part, seekers for the universal in art. However, the Objectivists, one of the central movements of this period, though clearly secular and not ethnic, had a membership that was entirely Jewish—Charles Reznikoff, Louis Zukovsky, Carl Rakosi, and George Oppen. Their shared cultural past influenced some of the poetics and much of the subject matter of their poetry. Indeed, one of the major proponents of this poetics, Charles Reznikoff, quite consciously described himself as a Jewish, American, urban poet. The recent complete collection of his poetry by Black Sparrow Press (1978) indicates the scope of Reznikoff's corpus. Even a quick perusal of his titles suggests the Jewish content of his poetry: "A Short History of Israel," "Kaddish," "The Fifth Book of the Maccabees," and *Holocaust*, for instance. But his Jewish influence is not merely a surface one of titles; the influence runs deep, in the themes and language of the individual poems. It is, however, a Jewishness of Objectivism, not Deep Imagism. His interest is quite in keeping with a rabbinic, rationalistic study of sources. Always distrustful of mysticism, Charles Reznikoff's sources are Bible, Talmud, and other rabbinic and historic texts, not *kabbalah*.

Reznikoff's knowledge of Jewish sources and of their contemporary meanings is seen, for instance, in "Glosses" (from *a Short History of Israel*) which begins with a comment on Moses's personal strength in deciding to become a shepherd, giving up the comfort of the Pharaoh's palace. For the Jew, the biblical Solomon as well as the biblical Moses do not exist merely in the past.[7] The poet writes

> As I sit in the street-car and hear the chatter about me,
> I do not envy Solomon
> who understood the language of birds as well.

Reznikoff must bear the extra knowledge that is typical of the Jew; he fears the greater perception, for the Jew's understanding is quite

different from the Gentile's. Yet each must learn from one another.
The Jew knows better than anyone else that denial is not necessarily
bad:

> Scorn
> shall be your meat
> instead of praise;
> you shall eat and eat of it
> all your days,
> and grow strong on it
> and live long on it, Jew
> You will not find it poison
> as the Gentiles do.[8]

Reznikoff's Jewishness also derives from post biblical history
and culture. For instance, in *By the Well of Living and Seeing*, Reznikoff remembers all the past anti-Semitic horrors of the exiled Jew.
He sees a "shambling boy" of a Jewish community and

> I looked at him in astonishment
> and thought: has nothing frightened you?
> Neither the capture of Jerusalem by the Babylonians, by Romans,
> by the Crusaders?
> No pogrom in Russia;
> no Nazi death-camp in Germany?
> How can you still go about so calmly?[9]

Along with painful images of Jewish history, Jewish art images appear in Reznikoff's memorializing of Jewishness. He speculates on
"Marc Chagall's picture of a green-faced Jew." In the painting there is
a book and a hanging:

> The hanging is green, too;
> embroidered on it, the shield of David
> and a single word in Hebrew, "hai,"
> meaning "life."
> When we moved, the moving-men dropped the picture
> and the glass that protected the print cracked;
> the crack ran over the word "hai"
> but the cracked glass held in the frame.[10]

Jewish history continues just as the print remains intact.

During the same historical period as the Objectivists, other Jewish-American poets followed a more academic mode, a mode similar to that in T. S. Eliot's *The Waste Land*. In fact, one of these poets, Hyam Plutzik, has written a telling appreciation of his idol, Eliot, in which the Jew cannot help but hold the master responsible for anti-Semitism, even as he admires Eliot for poetic inspiration. "For T. S. E. Only" begins "You called me a name on such and such a day—."[11] But Plutzik writes that he and Eliot could learn to accommodate themselves to one another because they both read Dante and they both hate Chicago. Plutzik invites Eliot to join him in weeping for their joint exile, suggesting that Eliot must expiate the sin of wit:

> I see your words wrung out in pain, but never
> The true compassion for creatures with you, that Dante
> Knew in his nine hells. O eagle! master!
> The eagle's ways of pride and scorn will not save
> Though the voice cries loud in humility. Thomas, Thomas,
> Come, let us pray together for our exile.
>
> You, hypocrite lecteur! mon semblable! mon frère!

The meditation on contemporary literary history acknowledges the value of the mode developed by Eliot even as it criticizes the man Eliot for his prejudice. Unlike Pound, of course, Eliot's anti-Semitism was not merely symbolic. Whereas Pound endorsed and mentored Jews such as Reznikoff, Rakosi, and Zukovsky, Eliot's anti-Semitism permeated his personal life as it did his poetry. Plutzik's poem finds Eliot's gentle nature a fraud, for the master could not turn it to Jews as well as to other humans. In this poem, we see one of the most poignant expressions of the conflict during this second era of Jewish-American poetry: how to be a poet and a Jew in the heyday of American Modernism; how to be true to both the universal ideals of the art object of the western tradition and the ethnic soul of the Jewish self.

The academic side of Jewish-American poetry, evident also in such poets as Delmore Schwartz and Karl Shapiro, is alive and well in contemporary America, the third historical era.[12] For instance, Howard Nemerov, John Hollander, Irving Feldman, and Anthony Hecht can be included in any list of important contemporary academic technicians of poetry, and these four writers have written important poems of Jewish content, theme, or form. Furthermore, these professorial types are beginning to manifest a change in attitude toward Jewish subjects and Jewish forms, a change found throughout contemporary Jewish-American Literature. There is an intensification of interest in things Jewish, even in the most esoteric of texts. Today, Anthony Hecht, the author of "Dover Bitch," that delightful parody of Matthew Arnold, writes poems like *Rites and Ceremonies*, a long poem on the presence of anti-Semitism in European history. And John Hollander, famous for his prosodic acrobatics, has written *Spectral Emanations*, a poem with images from the Lurianic *kabbalah*. These academic renditions of the intellectual's response to his Jewish past, combine with wide experiences in western culture so that the Jewish sources appear in a complex combination with multiple intellectual traditions. However, in both cases, the return to Jewish sources gives the poem an aura of comfort and the artist, perhaps, a pleasure in being home.

The contemporary academics join an essentially California-based group of Jewish poets (Jerome Rothenberg, David Meltzer, and Jack Hirshman) in their interest in the apocalyptic sources discussed in this book. Of these mystics manqués, Rothenberg is the most eclectic; his interest in Jewish subjects seems only partially an interest in discovering his Jewish sources and equally a part of his search for an accurate ethnopoetics. Hirschman turns to Jewish sources more in his search for a mystical answer to the destruction and pain of the Vietnam war; he and Allen Ginsberg ironically see Judaism as a mystical alternative to Christianity. The Jerusalem allusions in Hirschman are equally indebted to Blake, to the Bible, and to the Jewish symbol of Israel. These poets either consciously or unconsciously strive to define their Jewishness as a type of universal response, a means of communicating human experience. There seems to be a concerted effort not to seem parochial.

David Meltzer, on the other hand, a poetic counterpart to such fiction writers as Cynthia Ozick, Arthur A. Cohen, and Hugh

Nissenson, does not concern himself with being too Jewish. For these writers, if their audience is solely Jewish, they do not despair. They recognize that the only way for them to write honestly is to write with a Jewish past as foreground for the text. They feel, as any number of Christian esoterics have felt throughout the centuries, that if their readers are not willing to study the foreground then these readers will not be sympathetic to their themes. As Ozick has maintained, sometimes she just cannot express her points in English; sometimes she must use a "New Yiddish," a Judaicized English.

This change in attitude in the contemporary writer seems to coincide with a new identity in Jewish-American life. Since the end of World War II, there has been a great increase in the number of synagogues and temples and in their memberships. In the 1960s, this growth began to decline, but did not revert to pre-World War II numbers.[13] Furthermore, the growth in academic studies that are primarily Jewish (such as Holocaust courses, Yiddish language and literature courses, Hebrew language courses), indicates another population of Americans who are searching for a Jewish identity. Coinciding with the growth in other ethnic studies programs, Jewish-American studies programs and courses of the 1970s developed into a forum for personal identification that the college-age population seemed to crave. The success of these courses, particularly in English departments, was influenced by the growth in the number and quality of the writers who were producing literature that was essentially Jewish.

The poetry being discussed in this book is only a portion of the century-long history of Jewish-American poetry. The focus of this study is selective but centers on an important feature of today's Jewish and American literature. One facet that is essential in understanding the importance of contemporary Jewish-American poetry is the failure of its practitioners to fit the stereotype of Jewish-American literature (that is, rational, realistic fiction with an urban setting and a male point of view). Most obviously they are mystical or at least nonrational; there are a number of women poets; and they are poets, not novelists. The study of these writers, then, functions to open the canon, to establish a more accurate vision of Jewish-American literature.

Two other facets to this review are the variety and value of the poets discussed. In James Vinson's 1980 *Contemporary Poets* dictionary, all but three of the poets analyzed here at any length are included. Two of the three not included are women (which should not go unnoticed), women who have been associated with the Tree Book small press in California and its editors, Jerome Rothenberg, David Meltzer, and Jack Hirschman (these women are Susan Mernit and Rose Drachler). The other poet not included in Vinson is Howard Schwartz whose poetry is indeed not well known, but his position as an anthologist of the largest collection of contemporary Jewish poetry in English argues for his inclusion in my discussion, as he is almost creating the poetic canon. Furthermore, he is really quite a competent liturgical poet. Finally, two of the poets emphasized here (John Hollander and Jerome Rothenberg) represent important opposing forces on the contemporary poetry scene.

John Hollander and Jerome Rothenberg are important in themselves and as exemplary of the formalist/academic side of poetry on the one hand and the oral/avant-garde side of poetry on the other. John Hollander, currently a Yale professor of English, winner of *Poetry's* Levinson award (1974), and a Guggenheim recipient, is one of the few contemporary American poets included in the 1982 Magill *Critical Survey of Poetry*. Likened to Wallace Stevens by Harold Bloom,[14] Hollander is distrustful of the avant-garde and what he sees as anarchic contemporary poetry. As a critic, Hollander writes on Milton and English verse form. He argues that poetic freedom can only be found in the control of forms.[15] Jerome Rothenberg, imaginative anthologist and resurrector of lost literatures, coined the term "ethnopoetics," and then proceeded to create the discipline. Rothenberg sees ethnopoetics as a combination of vision and conflict, of speech and innovation, of past and present.[16] He defines the term as "a redefinition of poetry in terms of cultural specifics, with an emphasis on those alternative traditions to which the West gave names like 'pagan,' 'gentile,' 'tribal,' 'oral,' and 'ethnic.' "[17] Central to the Deep Image movement (associated with Diane Wakosi, Louis Simpson, Robert Bly, and James Wright), Rothenberg is a master of open forms, a significant force in counterpoetics and the avant-garde.

The other poets analyzed in this study include a 1960s child of the beat generation (Jack Hirschman); a master manipulator of point of view, noted for his academic Jewish verse (Irving Feldman); a combiner of myth and magic (David Meltzer); formalistic poets who write of the discomfort of being Jewish in the twentieth century (Robert Mezey and Harvey Shapiro); and Jewish feminists (Rose Drachler and Susan Mernit). This group contains exceptional poets in their own rights (whatever their reputations today, Meltzer and Drachler are inspired writers of distinctive poetry). Furthermore, the wide range of poets discussed suggests that this esoteric literature has touched all variety of Jewish poets writing in America. How truly remarkable it is to find a single source that has influenced poets as different as Rothenberg and Hollander.

The choice of which all these Jewish-American poets write is Muriel Rukeyser's nonchoice; refusing to be a Jew in the twentieth century is choosing "death of the spirit." These poets, like Rukeyser's accepting Jew, find

> The whole and fertile spirit as guarantee
> For every human freedom, suffering to be free,
> Daring to live for the impossible.[18]

Surely Rukeyser is here alluding to Lazarus's immigrants who came to the Mother of Exiles "yearning to breathe free." In the twentieth century the wish is accomplished, but suffering replaces yearning. The impossibility and the pain of being an eternal minority combine in the Jew and give him the power to endure and prevail in America. The Jewish-American poets capture the emotional truth in the beautiful difficulty of being a Jew in the twentieth century.

Chapter 1

Definitions And
Historic Contexts

Kabbalah has been a fertile subterrean influence on Jewish life since the beginning of the Jewish people. The term itself is associated with the medieval flowering of that esoteric culture, but the idea in its broadest sense, that is simply mystical tradition, has been present in almost all Jewish existence. My analysis of contemporary Jewish-American poetry stems from the study of messianism, a feature of Judaism that is particularly defined in this mystical tradition. Because messianism permeates Judaism in general, I have found it necessary to confine my concerns to a specific variety of Jewish messianism, messianism as communicated by the apocalyptic temper. Therefore, some major *kabbalistic* texts will not be discussed because they do not fit into this study's particular historical and conceptual framework. This framework originated with Gershom Scholem's assertion that apocalyptic messianism is a feature of the *kabbalah* only after the 1492 exile of the Sephardim.[1] Therefore, most of the movements referred to are of the sixteenth century or later, when the state of exile became most painful. After the end of the Golden Age of Spanish Jewry, all Jews knew that a good exile would be short-lived, that exile was not only the loss of homeland and autonomy, but also the loss of security and safety. However, two manifestations of messianism which predate this fifteenth-century marker are important in understanding Jewish apocalyptic messianism. These are: (1) the literature of the period

11

200 BCE–100CE, associated with the beginnings of Christianity, and with the Book of Daniel and the Enoch literature; and (2) the thirteenth-century Abulafian movement. The first is included because all apocalyptic literature is defined in reference to this period in which the genre flourished. The second is included because Abraham Abulafia, by calling himself Messiah and acting as one and by continuing to write prophetic texts, has to be considered an example of apocalyptic messianism within *kabbalah*. His brand of *kabbalah* did not become central to the mystical writings of Jews until the period Scholem identifies, but Abulafianism is a significant precursor. In this study, then, the literature of Jewish apocalyptic messianism represents a distinctively *kabbalistic* interpretation of historical catastrophe and messianic advent. The surprising influence of this medieval tradition on contemporary Jewish-American literature has significant sociological and cultural implications.

Stephen Sharot's recent analysis clarifies some of the sociological implications of apocalyptic messianism in three varieties of Jewish religious response: messianism, millenarianism, and magic. He indicates that in most instances, a religious movement combines these temperaments, but that certain historical and cultural features appear with Jewish millenarian fervor. He remarks that there was only one medieval episode of messianic activity among Ashkenazic Jews; in fact, the medieval Jewish appearances of millenarianism were Sephardic, in Spain, or, after 1492, in Italy.[2] Sharot does, however, find the prophetic *kabbalah* of Abulafia a significant development in Jewish mesianism. Sharot's analysis of apocalyptic movements describes in sociological terms as seminal the same movements I describe as seminal in other terms.

David Roskies, in *Against the Apocalypse*, writes solely of European Jewish authors, Ashkenazim. His argument provides an interesting counterpoint to mine: attention is on writing in Yiddish or Hebrew, not in English; his argument does not emphasize apocalyptic literature. He describes a long and complex tradition of Jewish response to catastrophe, both pogrom and Holocaust. These traditions include conscious irony, parody, and memorializing; in his scheme, apocalyptic writing is merely one traditional response to catastrophe. Indeed, Roskies (and apparently the writers of whom he writes) feels an aversion for the apocalyptic. In his opening chapter he writes:

> It now seems to me that to approach the abyss as closely as possible and to reach back over it in search of meaning, language, and song is a much more promising endeavor than to profess blind faith or apocalyptic despair. The alternative, to focus solely on the Event itself, succeeds only in robbing the dead of the fullness of their lives and in inviting the abstraction of the survivor into Everyman, the Holocaust into Everything.[3]

This desire to memorialize the individual is a moving resistance to allegorizing the Holocaust, the more specifically apocalyptic response to historical event. Roskies believes that though both rabbis and apocalyptists wrote of the past, the rabbis are "the implicit heroes of history" because they retained the specificity of event and actor.[4] The apocalyptists, instead, transformed event into a symbolic mode. Roskies, the rabbinic tradition, and most of the artists of which Roskies writes[5] find apocalyptic historiography insidious and unacceptable.[6] It is important that those exiled Jews who were farthest from the actuality of the Holocaust (Jews in America) would turn to the most esoteric and symbolic response to catastrophe and not those exiled Jews who were participants in that catastrophic event. Survivorship alone does not explain these opposing perspectives. David Roskies and his artists are more closely tied than the secular Jewish-American poets to the rabbinic mainstream that has suppressed for centuries the history of the Sabbatian movement and for millenia the mystical undercurrent in Jewish folklife. The discrepancies in influence on the poets discussed here and those he discusses become part of the weave in the counter-history that Gershom Scholem identified and defended as his life work. The difference in attitude toward the apocalyptic genre between the American-born poets and the European-born poets parallels the old conflict between *kabbalistic* Judaism and rabbinic Judaism. This difference also seems exacerbated by the one-hundred-year-old argument between the vigorous, Whitmanian, open-ended modes of America and the cultivated and formalistic modes of Europe. The disagreement between these two camps centers on nothing less than "what is poetry?" Furthermore, the Hebrew and Yiddish poets discussed in Roskies's book feel uncomfortable with anyone but survivors writing of the Holocaust. They accuse nonsurvivors' Holocaust poetry of inauthenticity and inaccuracy. The American writers, on the other hand, view their use of the apocalyptic as a means of elevating horror to cosmic significance and thereby honoring and sanctifying the martyrs within a religious historiography.

Jewish history, even counter-history, can be described as a commentary on a text, each current event being a reevaluation of a previous event; thereby, past and present combine in an uneasy coexistence. In usual cases, then, the present comes to be partially explicated by the past, often a biblical past where causation follows chronological order. However, when the event serving as foundation is of the messianic tradition, the explanation process is inverted, because causation is inverted. The Messiah's coming explains the present and the past. In an apocalyptic history (that is, a history with the messianic advent as a central feature), explanation is always future-oriented, the past explained in terms of the final event.[7] Such backward causation would seem negative to David Roskies, but to the apocalyptic temperament, it is an accurate philosophy of history.

A recent collection of messianic legends by the anthropologist Raphael Patai, suggests the popularity of the Messiah myth in contemporary intellectual circles. In the introduction to the collection, Patai describes the peculiar messianic chronology: "The Talmudic term denoting the events which precede the coming of the Redeemer is *'iqvot haMashiah*, literally, footprints of the Messiah. This is most significant because the Messianic advent is the only event in history which, although it has not yet come to pass, has left its footprints in advance in the soul of a people, and thereby shaped it and sustained it."[8]

A study of Jewish messianism's impact must focus on one particular rendition of that legend, otherwise it is too multifarious. Because of its surprising influence on contemporary Jewish-American letters, this study will use the messianic ideal as communicated through the most literary of devices—the apocalypse. This genre is especially apt for a contemporary Jewish literature because the apocalyptic is a genre associated with the exile and because it is associated with times of great upheaval and distress of the Jewish people. Post-Holocaust American literature by Jews is surely a literature of the exile and indicates (in the last twenty years) an awareness of the horrors of the Holocaust. Furthermore, the literature of the more rationalized manifestations of messianism which flourished during the nineteenth century (for example, Zionism, Reform Judaism, and Socialism) are devoid of the literary devices of the apocalypse, and contemporary Jewish-American poetry is quite consciously literary. In addition, rationalized notions of Jewish messianism avoid the discussion of contemporary chaos and decadence, the essential pessimism concerning the present state of things, and supernatural elements such as resurrection of the dead, God's overt involvement in history, and angelogy—all characteristics of apocalyptic literature and of the poetry discussed here.

In *The Sense of an Ending*, Frank Kermode cites certain feelings and atmospheres entailed in secular literary apocalypse: terror, decadence, renovation, transition and/or scepticism.[9] In addition to these qualities, the modern apocalypse exhibits factors and literary patterns found in that genre called biblical and neo-Hebraic apocalyptic literature. Literary critics should be most sensitive to these features, but have not been. According to D. H. Lawrence, a not entirely unsympathetic reader of apocalyptic, the creation of this particular literature is closely tied to the time in which it first developed—the intertestamental period from 200 BCE to 100 CE. After the destruction of the Temple and the disappearance of prophecy, Lawrence feels that "[t]he Jews became a people of *postponed destiny*." Visions, favorite apocalyptic modes of divine communication, became some of God's most frequent devices of communication with his people.[10] Despite Lawrence's biased version of the Jewish tradition, he identifies a significant element in the apocalypse—the delayed gratification of the exile. The goal is known, but the time it will take to reach that goal is not; the end of time explains the process towards that end. The successful and complete end of the exile, the new kingdom of Israel, will not merely be a mirror of the original kingdom, but an entirely new order. Jewish powerlessness and degradation only grew over the centuries of the *goles*, with each period of tolerance being shown for what it was—a temporary mask of the beast of anti-Semitism. Immediately after the Golden Age of Spanish Jewry, in the late fifteenth and early sixteenth centuries, came the Spanish Inquisition; and after the nineteenth-century *Haskalah*, in 1939–1945, the Holocaust. In this historical context, the comfortable American exile has frightening implications. The literary device that suggests delayed gratification, pessimism about the material world, symbolic interpretation of historical events, and visionary reworking of the present status would therefore become a logical choice for Jewish writers in contemporary society. In fact, the apocalyptic, associated from its inception with times of spiritual crisis of the Jewish people, has appeared most significantly at the periods of catastrophe for the Jewish people. The Bar Kochba defeat preceded the apocalyptic of the later noncanonical Hebraic texts. The sixteenth-century Sephardic community, in the shadow of the Inquisition, produced the apocalyptic literature associated with the Lurianic *kabbalah* and later the Shabbatian movement. In contemporary secular times, in the United States, a community essentially protected from the horrors of the Holocaust and World War II, the contemporary literature of Jewish-Americans returns to apocalyptic patterns, theories, and devices. As described here, apocalyptic is a theory of language as well as a cosmology, eschatology, and theology. The *kabbalistic* and even the rational Talmudic attitudes toward *tanakh* are clearly in keeping with this elevation of the word and the letter to meditative significance. The contemporary writers most influenced by this Hebraic investigation of the word and the letter, therefore, are not surprisingly poets, the most self-conscious of our contemporary wordsmiths.

Contemporary literature by Jewish Americans must be understood in the context of the classical apocalyptic genre as defined by biblical scholars who write of its first flourishing, 200 BCE to 100 CE. Interestingly enough, the larger number of those who write perceptively of this literature are Christian. Granted, their basic premise is progressive revelation and they invariably overemphasize the superhuman qualities of the individual messiah figure

that appears in apocalyptic literature and provide a Christian interpretation (that is, individualized) of the ideal of suffering servant (in
Judaism, of course, that is the people Israel). But because of a prejudice in Jewish scholarship from the *Haskalah* to the present,
mystical and symbolic aspects of Judaism have not been granted full
attention. And the apocalyptic is always symbolic and usually
mystical. Not until Gershom Scholem turned the scientific principles of *Haskalah* to the study of *kabbalah* and false messiahs did the
intellectual Jewish community rediscover what the folk culture knew
all along: that the apocalyptic was alive and well in Judaism and had
been since 200 BCE, and perhaps since even earlier than that. In
fact, the biblical scholar Stanley Brice Frost's *Old Testament
Apocalyptic: Its Origin and Growth* identifies passages in Ezekiel,
Zechariah, Joel, and Isaiah as well as the entire Book of Daniel as
examples of the apocalyptic temper and literary tradition in *tanakh.*

According to Frost, in canonical or noncanonical literature the
combination of myth (primitive poetry, philosophy, speculation)
and eschatology (the study of the final event, whether that event be
perceived as *in* history or *of* history) is the apocalyptic.[11] Frost
analyzes several myths that are characteristic of the primitive
Hebrew faith and develops the transformation of these myths by the
sophistication of the *Yahwehist.* This transformation combines
history and eschatology and culminates in the creation of the Jewish
people.[12] A most important aspect of the apocalyptic is messianism,
which Frost associates with rebirth and creation ideas from the
original Hebraic faith, only becoming eschatological at the time of
the exile.[13] The messianic idea has always been associated with the
contemporary political and historical situation of the Jews.
Therefore, first the Messiah was equated with the contemporary
reigning king, then he was identified as the offspring of the house of
David; in the apocalyptic he was placed in a messianic age, an
eschatological conclusion.[14] In Frost's words, "Messianism, then is
the eschatologizing of the enthronement cult just as apocalyptic is
the eschatologizing of the old cosmology myths."[15] The apocalyptists do not deny, but rather transform, history and historical thinking; in a reversion to mythic thinking, the apocalyptists mythologize
history.[16] Apocalyptic messianism combines unusual habits of mind:

conflating history's chronological causation with myth's eternal patterns and eschatology's backward causation.

The apocalyptic genre is characterized by particular goals and purposes. For instance, Joshua Block, former head librarian of the Judaica collection of the New York Public Library, indicates that the aspects of the apocalyptic that are often described as predictive are in fact merely symbols used to develop a theocratic interpretation of history.[17] Apocalyptic, then, explains God's hand in history. According to Mr. Frost, the apocalyptic protests;[18] it protests against the political, social, moral, and spiritual situation of being in exile. Clearly identified with the loss of place, the loss of power, and the loss of self-determination for the Jewish people, the apocalyptic speaks for an exile group threatened by the powerful and irrational forces of the material world, but it speaks in a highly symbolic fashion that can be understood only by the initiates, even as it reveals the secrets of the universe, God, and their own mission. It is, by definition, a literature of the occult. It is by necessity, abstruse and ambiguous. In fact, then, one purpose of the literature is to communicate secret information only to the specially trained.

Pessimistic optimism, dualism, and a distinctive historiography are other characteristic features of this secret symbolic communication. First, the apocalyptic combines pessimism concerning the present historical and political situation with optimism about God's eventual positive intervention in history in Israel's behalf (a clear indication of the nationalistic temper of Jewish apocalyptic). In several versions of messianism, in fact, the positive features of the messianic age are not extended to the Gentile. Second, the senses of creation and of time are dualistic in this literature. Evil (often aligned with the Gentile, worldly powers), a very real power, wages war against God and His people, and the time man knows now opposes the time during the Messianic Age. As a direct result of this dualism, a well-defined angelology and demonology commonly appears in apocalyptic literature. Third, the idea of history in the apocalyptic blends a theodicy with a dependence on past tradition in Jewish history. Therefore, the apocalyptic joins historical retrospectives with a cosmological view of history. The content of time becomes more significant than the chronology of history.[19] In fact, the apocalyptic unites history and cosmology.[20] The guise of prophecy is just that—a guise. According to some biblical scholars, the apocalyptist pretends inspiration and depends on pseudoecstacy.[21] Such pretention elevates the secular criticism of the contemporary world to an eternal and cosmic realm. The patterns of history presented in apocalyptic retrospectives argue different epochs in history and different qualities of time. For instance, different ages echo different political powers in control of the world's history. All of these discrete ages contrast with that age to come, the age of the Messiah. The aspect of that age to come probably most emphasized by the Christian critics, resurrection, and its preceding event, judgment, appear in the traditional Jewish concept of the Messianic Age, but not nearly as significantly, nor as doctrinally absolute as in Christianity.

Several literary characteristics of the apocalyptic come as direct consequences of the attitudes just described. First, mythic patterns become literary devices in the apocalyptic. The conflict between the powers of good and evil, the creation out of nothingness, the Golden Age which parallels the Messianic Age, the judgment and its day of terror, and the anointed one who will guide us in the time of terror and in the time of peace, all figure prominently in the literature. Second, symbolism, often based on these ancient myths, animal imagery, or numerology, abounds in the apocalyptic. Third, the literature shows a predilection for esoteric information transmitted to the human through angels, biblical characters, visions, or dreams. Visions themselves explain part of the supernatural quality of the literature, but so does the presence of semimagical, semidivine creatures like Isaiah, Elijah, and Enoch. Fourth, most of this literature is pseudonymous or anonymous. By using the names of characters noted for their prophecy or wisdom, the apocalyptist could invest his writing and interpretation of current events with the special authority of ancient tradition. Further, pseudonymity helps explain notorious historical inaccuracies of the apocalyptic and the strange unhistorical historical sense of the literature. Not the chronology but the quality of the event, the relationship of that event to the *eschaton* provides meaning for apocalyptic history. Finally, Frost suggests an alternation of literary styles in the apocalyptic—an alternation between lyric poetry and prophetic rhetoric.[22]

Several book-length studies discuss the relationship of

apocalyptic to secular literature and to Jewish literary history (for example, the D. H. Lawrence and Frank Kermode books). John R. May, in *Toward a New Earth*, writes of the apocalyptic in the American novel. His definition, a specifically Christian one, identifies the apocalyptic sense of time, unifying past, present, and future,[23] and the pattern of catastrophe and renewal, typical of Jewish apocalyptic literature and essential to an understanding of the apocalyptic influence on contemporary Jewish-American poetry. In his book on Jewish apocalyptic literature Joshua Bloch describes the apocalyptic as a Jewish genre, comparing the supplementation of the genre to that of the Talmud.[24] History and fiction did not represent opposing modes of interpretation. Age, not the individual author, mattered; so long as a document was old, it had authority.[25] Bloch compares his age's secular fiction with the apocalyptic of 200 BCE in its suggestiveness and its unification of the present and the future.[26] He writes that particularly similar are the apocalyptic and the historical/religious novel of his day "by which the doctrines of a later epoch are put into the mouths of historical characters, not so much with a view to deceiving the reader as with the hope of winning a greater acceptance for these views by the seductive association."[27] Whatever the subject matter of an historical novel, Bloch seems to indicate, the attitude toward history is an apocalyptic one. When the historical subject itself is a messianic movement, the apocalyptic sense of history is reenforced as the second chapter and conclusion of this study will suggest. More recently, Harold Bloom has recognized the relationship of the apocalyptic to secular literature. In *Kabbalah and Criticism* (New York: Seabury Press, 1975), he defines the pattern of tradition and the creative revision of tradition in the *kabbalistic* schools. However, his theoretical emphasis encourages him to overlook the most obvious indications of influence—that is, direct reference to apocalyptic literature, messianic aspirants, and messianic speculation. In recent poetry, many such references appear.

Probably one of the most important aspects of the apocalyptic is the tradition of messianism. Here myth and history join most excitingly: the legends of the anointed one come together with some highly visible and powerful historical figures who have at different periods presented themselves as the Messiah. Even in liturgy, messianism assumed a central position. In the closest thing to a credo ever formulated by Jewish philosophers, Moses Maimonides's *Thirteen Principles of the Faith*, the last principle reads: "I believe with a complete faith in the coming of the Messiah; and even though he tarry, nevertheless I await him every day that he should come." Canonical and noncanonical sources provide traditions that attach themselves to the Jewish notion of Messiah. Remembering the earlier statement in this chapter, that all of Jewish history can be seen as a commentary on a text, will remind the reader of the method whereby this most vital of traditions has become transformed, developed, and enriched over the millenia. The messianic myth and its concomittant and parallel mysticism and supernaturalism, its apocalyptic visions, remained part of the Jewish folkways and folk wisdom even when the German rationalists denied its existence. Joseph Sarachek, in *The Doctrine of the Messiah in Medieval Jewish Literature*, finds much of the rabbinic notion of the Messiah in the prophetic books of the Bible. However, some features of messianism that will interest us here can only be found in the later literature—the idea of a redeemer Messiah, the inevitability of the coming of positive features of the future age, the concept of a Messiah ben Joseph who will die in the chaos before the age of peace, the esoteric practice of calculating the date of the coming of the Messiah, and finally the association of the Messiah with the end of time.[28] These later features, associated with apocalyptic messianism, are also found in some of the poetry of contemporary Jewish Americans.

The Jewish Messiah is, in rabbinic or apocalyptic literature, the one anointed by God, but he is not divine. God gives him savior qualities which are in keeping with human powers as invested in specially blessed individuals. As representative of the people Israel, the Jewish Messiah functions as Every Jew. Dividing Messiah into two characters (the Messiah ben Joseph who will lead the forces of righteousness in the final conflict that precedes the judgment and the end of time, the conflict during which he will be killed, and the Messiah ben David, the offspring of the house of David, who will rule during the Messianic Age) provides the people with a military and a spiritual leader. Furthermore, the division suggests the peculiar combination of historical individual and mythic type that characterizes the Jewish Messiah. Aided by another biblical prototype, the Jewish Messiah further contrasts with the Christian concept by depending on assistance from an Elijah-like prophet. Historical manifestations of this prophet include the figures of Rabbi Akiba and his celebration of Bar Kochba, Hayyim Vital and his writings of the philosophies of Isaac Luria, and Nathan of Gaza and his relationship to Shabbatai Zevi. These spokesmen attempt to awaken Israel to the messiahship of their respective leaders. If the awakening is successful, Gentiles will follow Israel, assuming Judaism as the one true relationship with God. This conversion will usher in the utopianism of the Messianic Age, a time of the ingathering of the exiles, and the resurrection of the dead (sometimes through the services of Messiah, but usually through the power of God alone). Before this great time of peace, however, comes a time of war, chaos and destruction, often called the "pangs of the Messiah." This episode in the history of the Jewish Messiah allowed any period of special stress for the Jewish people to become the foundation for a new spate of apocalyptic speculation.

The Messiah, according to Jewish legend, is eternal; he existed prior to creation, but he must wait until his appointed time to reappear on earth. In Bird's Nest, a refuge in Eden, he awaits his call in meditation and sorrow. Because the wait for the Messiah was painful, there arose in the Jewish tradition a rich esoterica for calculating the messianic advent. There also developed a traditon in *kabbalah* of manipulating these speculations and a special *gnosis* characteristic of the apocalyptic symbolism used to hasten the coming of Messiah. Such philosophy culminated in some of the most destructive events of Jewish history. Shabbatianism and Frankism, however dangerous, based their antinomianism on the ancient speculation on the transformation of Torah in the Messianic Age. In the new age there had to be a new Torah, a new law.

The apocalyptic itself as a literary genre becomes a causal factor in some movements of pseudomessiahs. Abba Hillel Silver, in *A History of Messianic Speculation in Israel*, states that some of the individuals were created as much by the literary documents of apocalypse as they were by political and social situations.[29] In Jewish apocalyptic messianism, therefore, literature can create reality. No tradition valued the power of the word more. However, the natural reticence of the apocalyptists in committing to writing the secrets of the time and the nature of the Messianic Age resulted in very few intelligible texts being extant. A very few, highly symbolic, indeed obscurely symbolic, renderings of the theories of apocalyptic messianism and several more straightforward renderings written by disciples rather than leaders of movements do exist. The documents do not provide a shared doctrine of apocalyptic messianism. Rather, each distinctive theology working within the larger tradition of Jewish messianism develops its own particular emphasis. Therefore we will best be able to see the impact of apocalyptic messianism on contemporary Jewish-American poetry by distinguishing several schools of Jewish apocalyptic literature and describing the most important features of these schools.

The apocalyptic appears in portions of the Bible as sections or visions in the books of Ezekiel, Isaiah, Zechariah, and Joel, but the earliest examples of fully worked apocalypse coincide with the assimilation into the Judaic tradition of the idea of exile and loss of homeland. Though the first Temple had been destroyed in the sixth century and the Babylonian captivity became the prototype for the Jew's exilic existence, it took almost five centuries for the pattern of homelessness to seem the norm. Apocalyptic is a literary genre that accepts the exile. The two examples most characteristic and most influential from the early period are the Book of Daniel and the Book of Enoch.

Written about 165 BCE, but set in the sixth century BCE, the Book of Daniel typifies the apocalyptic—highly symbolic, visionary, mystical, pseudonymous, dualistic, deterministic, and complete with an angelic visitation and God's direct intervention in Israel's history. The two passages of this only canonical apocalyptic book that develop the messianic aspects most thoroughly are chapters 7:13–14 and 9:25–27. Interestingly enough, one is clearly poetry, and the other clearly prose, suggesting that Frost's impression of stylistic alternation is quite ancient. One passage tells of the qualities of the messianic character, the other of the fate of the anointed one.

Both are parts of the visions allowed Daniel and explicated for him by angelic forces. The first,

> I saw in the night visions,
> And, behold, there came with the clouds of heaven
> One like unto a son of man,
> And he came even to the Ancient of days,
> And he was brought near before Him.
> And there was given him dominion,
> And glory, and a kingdom,
> That all the peoples, nations, and languages
> Should serve him;
> His dominion is an everlasting dominion, which shall not
> pass away.
> And his kingdom that which shall not be destroyed.[30]

This passage presents the Jewish relationship of God to a clearly human Messiah. All powers, direct gifts of God, are eternal and indestructible. In the later passage,

> Know therefore and discern, that from the going forth of the word
> to restore and to build Jerusalem unto one anointed, a prince,
> shall be seven weeks; and for threescore and two weeks, it shall
> be built again, with broad place and moat, but in troublous times.
> And after the threescore and two weeks shall an anointed one be
> cut off, and be no more; and the people of a prince that shall
> come shall destroy the city and the sanctuary; but his end shall be
> with a flood; and unto the end of the war desolations are deter-
> mined. And he shall make a firm covenant with many for one
> week; and for half of the week he shall cause the sacrifice and the
> offering to cease; and upon the wing of detestable things shall be
> that which causeth appalment; and that until the extermination
> wholly determined be poured out upon that which causeth appal-
> ment.

The interpretation of the numbers in this particular passage has funded much of the speculation of biblical scholars on the date of the coming of the Messiah. Here, chaotic times precede the messianic advent and the death and implied return of the Messiah. Symbolic time periods, in this section and in other sections of the Book of Daniel, suggest the history of man as divided into historical ages, each age associated with another Gentile power and with another quality of time.

The Book of Enoch, a second example of early apocalyptic, is actually a compendium of literature, with the earliest passages being dated earlier than the Book of Daniel and the later parts being written as recently as 105–64 BCE. As a collection from different hands over a lengthy period, perhaps as long as a century, the Book of Enoch does not present a consistent theory of the Messiah. In fact, there are contradictory theories of the Messiah in the literature. The misconception that this particular compendium had no effect on Jewish thought hinges on two factors: the strange history of the text and the over simplified contrast of Judaism as rationality and Christianity as mysticism. Though the Book of Enoch enjoyed great popularity for several centuries after its creation, it fell into disrepute by the fourth century CE and an extant text was not discovered until the nineteenth-century discovery of an Ethiopic manuscript. The single most convincing proof that despite this absence of a text, the Book of Enoch was known in Jewish circles is the *Pirke de Rabbi Eliezer*, a very popular eighth-century *aggada* which contains direct quotations from the Book of Enoch. There are several manuscripts of this *Pirke* extant and numerous editions published since the first edition in 1514. Several major Hebrew theological treatises refer to the *Pirke de Rabbi Eliezer*. Therefore, through the auspices of this eighth-century piece, the Book of Enoch was preserved for the Jewish tradition.[31]

In the Enoch literature, the Messiah assumes more than human powers. Though his power, particularly his judgmental powers, are allowed him by God, the Enoch Messiah begins to take dominion over all things, including all destruction. Called by several names in Enoch: the "Righteous One," the "Elect One," "His Anointed," "My [God's] Son," he is most often "that Son of Man." He existed prior to creation, he is privy to God's wisdom which he imparts to man, and he dwells with and rules the righteous, the elect, of God. These righteous persons will partake of the messianic banquet and therefore will

. . . lie down and rise up for ever and ever.
And the righteous and elect shall have risen from the earth,
and ceased to be of downcast countenance (62:14–15).[32]

The Messiah becomes capable of magical acts: "the Righteous and Elect One shall cause the house of his congregation to appear" (53:6). Enoch's vision of the New Jerusalem, in chapter 90, is prototypical:

> And I saw that a white bull was born, with large horns, and all the beasts of the field and all the birds of the air feared him and made petition to him all the time. And I saw till all their generations were transformed, and they all became white bulls; and the first among them became a lamb, and that lamb became a great animal and had great black horns on its head; and the Lord of the sheep rejoiced over it and over all the oxen. And I slept in their midst: and I awoke and saw everything. This is the vision which I saw while I slept, and I awoke and blessed the Lord of righteousness and gave Him glory.

The Messiah, though human, attains great power and leadership through the auspices of God. Also visions and symbolism, particularly animal symbolism, so typical of the apocalyptic, pervade this passage.

Two basic concepts of the apocalyptic mark these two early texts. First, historical patterns, symbolic eras, must be followed in the predetermined chronology leading toward the messianic advent. Biblical historical events, particularly the exile, become prototypes for all history to follow. Just as Jewish history is seen as a commentary on a text, so the individual's autobiography becomes a prototype for the Jewish people, for in Judaism the individual Jew represents the people. Second, angels in the early apocalyptic become autonomous beings with names, functions, and distinct personalities. They function either to interpret symbolic visions or to give symbolic visions to initiated humans. Enoch himself appears as a holy man who, by virtue of his assumption into heaven, partakes of semidivine qualities. In apocalyptic literature and the *kabbalah* one of the most important traditions of the Enoch legends concerns his transformation into the angel Metatron, an angel who is sometimes called the "lesser YHVH."[33]

The second manifestation of apocalyptic messianism to show a significant influence on contemporary Jewish-American poetry is the thirteenth-century *kabbalah* of Abraham Abulafia, which emphasizes the mystical value of the Hebrew language. The Hebrew alphabet as a key to the mystery of God's creation had been defined in the ninth-century *Sepher Yetsirah*, a source for Abulafia's theories. The twenty-two Hebrew letters plus the ten *sephira* (faces of God) provide the thirty-two paths to wisdom because they form the foundation for creation. The *Sepher Yetsirah* divides the Hebrew alphabet into three types of letters with differing phonological, pictorial, symbolic, and mystical significances. Abulafia's *kabbalah* went further than his source by arguing a meditative technique that could produce a prophetic and ecstatic experience for the initiate. In fact, the Abulafian prophet could attain the position of Messiah, a role that Abraham Abulafia assumed for himself when in 1280 he journeyed to Rome to influence Pope Nicholas III to reconsider his attitude toward the Jews.

Abulafia's attraction for the contemporary Jewish-American poet lies in his spectacular life history as well as his doctrines on the study of the Hebrew language. Abulafia's *kabbalah* combines the most mystical and the most rational aspects of Jewish tradition. Along with the *Sepher Yetsirah* and the tracts of the German Hasid Eleazer of Worms, Abulafia studied Moses Maimonides. When Abraham Abulafia guided his disciples into the meditation on God's names, he quite consciously chose the most abstract of abstractions for meditative consideration in order to avoid the confusion of material creation. Torah is creation itself and if both, Torah and creation, are merely extended presentations of the names of God, then the reason for Abulafia's interest in the numerous names of God as meditative subjects is quite clear. The letters of the alphabet are merely another manifestation of God.

Abulafia's particular *kabbalah* depends on the tradition of numerical and symbolical meaning invested in the Hebrew letters: *gematria* (the numerical value of the letters of the Hebrew alphabet), *notarikon* (the perception of letters in a word as acrostics for sentences), and *zeruf* (the permutations of letters to produce different words, or combinations of letters). According to a disciple's description of the Abulafian path, the effect on the individual evolves as the student's meditation on the letters and on God's names deepens. He studies the "Great Name of God, consisting of seventy-two names," when emotions and ecstatic terror overcome him: "the letters took on in my eyes the shape of great mountains, strong trembling seized me and I could summon no strength, my hair stood on end, and it was as if I were not in this world."[34] The seventy-two names are also denoted by "the seventy-two lettered name of God," the most important single name of God for Abulafia's system of meditation. He created for his disciples two hundred meditative circles based on this idea of the seventy-two lettered name and the seventy-two names. The significance of seventy-two has three important explications. First, the seventy-two lettered name of God has been described as the combination of the letters that make up the names of the twelve tribes of Israel, the three patriarchs, and the nine-letter phrase *shivtei Yisroel* (tribes of Israel). Second, the name has been described as the numerical value of the Ineffable Name, that is the tetragram, when the four letters (*yod he vov he*) are spelt out with the letter *yod* being used as the filling out of the individual letters *he* and *aleph* for *vov*. Third, and most important to Abulafia, is the derivation of the seventy-two three-letter combinations from the three verses of Exodus 14:19–21. Each of these verses has seventy-two letters. A table of the seventy-two triple letters created by reading verse nineteen forward, verse twenty backward, and verse twenty-one forward was the foundation of Abulafian *kabbalah*. In each of these *kabbalistic* descriptions, reality hides behind individual letters and combinations of letters.

In order to attain ecstacy, the individual had to follow three levels of cleansing in the meditation. First the body had to be cleansed, then the bodily disposition (especially the disposition toward anger) had to be cleansed, and finally the soul had to be cleansed of knowledge of all other sciences. According to Abraham Abulafia, the only way to attain such *kabbalistic* heights of meditation was to choose as the subject of meditation the abstraction of abstractions—God's names. In *Haye Olam Ha-Ba*, Abulafia compares the process to music: "You will whirl the letters front and back and create many melodies." After a period of fear and trembling, the initiate will sense God's presence, His wisdom: "This will occur as though his body had been anointed from head to toe with oil and ointment. And he will be messiah to God, his very messenger, and will be called the Angel of God. And his name shall be like the name of his teacher, Shaddai, who shall name him Mattat, Minister of the Interior."[35]

For those not schooled in *gematria*, *notarikon*, and *zeruf*, Abulafia's manuals of meditation, including the circles of meditation and the definition of prophecy, are the more comprehensible of his writings. But it is his prophetic, apocalyptic piece (he wrote twenty-six according to his own account, but only the one has survived), *Sepher Ha-Ot*, that is the most startling example of his writing. This book defies literal translation and, even under the best of circumstances, remains obscure to the modern mind. However, this thirteenth-century apocalypse best illustrates the tradition of apocalyptic messianism according to Abulafia and best reveals the influence of Abulafia on contemporary Jewish-American poets. In this tract, Abulafia, using the name Zechariah which, along with Raziel, bears the same numerical value as his family name, promises to reveal to his disciples the true nature of the name of God. Characteristic of apocalyptic writing, Abulafia's treatise reveals secrets of the universe under the guise of a pseudonym of ancient authority. The great name developed from the three verses in Exodus is given in its entirety in section two of *Sepher Ha-Ot* and the four letters of the tetragram are permutated throughout the piece. Recognizing himself as the messenger, the anointed of God, Abulafia writes an apocalypse in the Jewish tradition. The esoteric number symbolism is reenforced by speculations on the date of the coming of the Messiah, visions of destruction, warnings of the result of failing to maintain secrecy, and the eras of predetermined time which end with the rule of Messiah.[36] All of these symbolic referents are typical of classical apocalyptic literature.

In 1976, a group of California-based poets collected writings of Abulafia to be published as a Tree Text (the collection cited so far in the analysis of Abulafia's *kabbalah*). David Meltzer was the editor as well as the translator of several of the pieces. Jack Hirschman was a translator, most particularly of *Sepher Ha-Ot*, which in his translation becomes a poem by Jack Hirschman as well as a translation of an apocalypse by Abraham Abulafia. In that same year, David Meltzer edited a collection of *kabbalistic* texts for Seabury Press which included the texts from *The Path of the Names*, and, in 1978 Jerome Rothenberg, in his *A Big Jewish Book*, included annotated examples of Abulafia's meditative circles as well as excerpts from Abulafia's other writings. Not surprisingly, Meltzer, Hirschman, and Rothenberg frequently refer to Abulafia in their poetry. Hirschman has not given his readers helpful comments in notes or introductions as to his understanding of the Abulafian *kabbalah*, as have Meltzer and Rothenberg. Rothenberg describes Abulafia's *kabbalah* as a sort of "medieval lettrism," thereby introducing his readers to a comparison of Abulafia's religious meditative technique with some twentieth-century poetic attitudes toward language. He describes the movement of sound and meditation from letter to letter, *dilug* and *kefitsah*, skipping and jumping (Abulafia's terms). Such a process explains the adumbration of meaning by mystical meditation on letters.[37] Rothenberg also seems deeply influenced by Abulafia's life, a life that included a messianic zeal so strong that Abulafia traveled to Rome to convert the Pope. In the collection of Abulafian writings Meltzer edited, *The Path of the Names*, Meltzer gives a conventional description of Abulafia's *kabbalah*. For Meltzer, the sound of the words—not of individual letters, but of individual words—should allow the proper *kavanah* (intention) in the creation of poetry. In an earlier collection of *kabbalistic* texts, Meltzer compares *kabbalah* to poetry in its "study of and submission to the mysteries of the world." For Meltzer, the complexity of the mystical tradition lies in its status beyond the written word, so that texts are compared to "shadows" or "ghosts" rather than facts. The creation on paper is the result of meditation and is an attempt to penetrate the phenomenal universe.[38] Furthermore, for both Meltzer and Rothenberg, the Abulafian prophetic *kabbalah*, with all its messianic allusions, becomes one of the primary features of the two poets' descriptions of the role of the poet. In the contemporary Jewish-American poet's mind, then, Abraham Abulafia, with his attention to the letter and the word, functions as an inspiration for poetry. The third manifestation of the apocalyptic to be influential on contemporary poetry, the Lurianic school, was an understandable result of the shock and horror felt by the Jewish community after the expulsion of the Jews from Spain in 1492. No earlier exile had been as comfortable for Jews as the Spanish exile during the preceding era, the Golden Age of Spanish Jewry. The psychological trauma of the Jewish exile became even more painfully real when these privileged Jews were thrown out of the country that had been their home for generations. Before this expulsion, according to Gershom Scholem, the *kabbalists* were "a small group of esoterics who had little desire to spread their ideas, and who would have been the last to promote any movement for introducing radical changes into Jewish life, or for altering its rhythms."[39] Highly individualized and meditative, the older *kabbalah* studied the creation, not the final event of cosmogony. However, after the 1492 catastrophe, a new messianic mode inspired *kabbalists* to see in the outline of the beginning, the foundations of the end. Their view became apocalyptic.

The Lurianic *kabbalah* is the creation of a group of sixteenth-century mystics from the town of Safed in Palestine.[40] Isaac Luria (1534–1572), not a prolific writer nor a particularly systematic thinker, inspired this school of mystics; he assumed the role of *zaddik*. Very well educated in the rabbinic literature and the *kabbalistic* commentary (especially the *Zohar* and the work of his contemporary Moses Cordovero), Luria perceived of himself as a great innovator. In fact, he identified himself as the Messiah ben Joseph. Most of his disciples and certainly his major follower, Hayyim Vital, identifed Luria as the Messiah. Vital's evaluation is particularly significant since his writings are the major documents of the Lurianic *kabbalah*. This *kabbalah* is a complex, thorough, and highly imaginative theosophy, cosmogony, and cosmography.

The three major elements of the Lurianic *kabbalah* that appear in the poetry of contemporary Jewish-American poets are the theory of emanations, the cosmogonic myth of *tsimtsim, shevirah ha-Kelim, tikkun*, and the female principle of God, *Shekinah*. The relationship between the cosmogonic myth and the more ancient theory of emanations is perhaps the most creative change of the Lurianic *kabbalah*. Emanation of God (or the *Ein Sof*) into the world had been argued since the first *kabbalistic* text and school. Whether or not the emanation was identical or distinct from the emanator, whether the process of emanation was a temporal sequence or not, that emanation began with an aspect of *Ein Sof*; it began with an act of the will of the prime cause to do something in the world. The Lurianic *kabbalah* changed two major aspects of the tradition. First, the creation begins with *Ein Sof's* retreat, not his active emanation. Second, the first containment of *Ein Sof* is not an emanation, but is *Adam Kadmon*, a new intermediary function between *Ein Sof* and the world of emanation. According to the cosmogonic myth of the Lurianic school, God must withdraw into himself in order for there to be room for creation. This contraction also explains the separation of the *Shekinah* from the male principle of God. She becomes exiled from Him in a fashion similar to the exile of the Jewish people. After God's withdrawal (*tsimtsim*), His light fills the space provided and forms the primordial man, *Adam Kadmon*. Light, which should be preserved, flows out of the new configuration; however, the vessels provided for the preservation are frail and they break (*shevirah ha-Kelim*). Sparks and pieces of vessels fall from the original stasis. The parts of *Adam Kadmon* represent different faces (*sefira*) of God, and in fact, are broken in different degrees. These differences are a consequence of the status of the emanation to which the individual *sephiroth* relates. The closer the emanation to *Ein Sof*, the less broken its corresponding *sephiroth*. The exiled *Shekinah* is part of this fallen state, in Scholem's words, "a genuine symbol of the 'broken' state of things in the realm of divine potentialities."[41] Returning the sparks to the repaired vessels (*tikkun*) is the spiritual duty of all man, a messianic action that will return not only the people to Eretz Yisroel, but also will reunite *Shekinah* with God. As a *kabbalistic* comment on exile and redemption, the Lurianic *kabbalah* explains something that is true both of the divinity and of man's role in the correction of the present order. Man is given new moral stature; he becomes "the ideal of the ascetic whose aim is the Messianic reformation, the extinction of the world's blemish, the restitution of all things in God—the man of spiritual action who through the *Tikkun* breaks the exile, the historical exile of the Community of Israel and that inner exile in which all creation groans."⁴²

Although the idea of emanation is as ancient as *kabbalah*, the Lurianic school articulates the most sophisticated and complex version. Furthermore, the Lurianic version of emanation took on the messianic qualities in the Lurianic *kabbalah* and has shown the most significant influence on the symbols of emanations in contemporary Jewish-American poetry. Because of the all-inclusive nature of Lurianic emanations, the poems most influenced by this theory are long poems. In fact, true to the symbol of the many in one, these long poems are long expressions of the presence of soul or spirituality in the world in the form of multisection poems. The poets argue for a basic but not easily apparent principle of oneness, a unity, and a foundation.

The other manifestations of messianism to be discussed in this study include the spectacular lives of Shabbatai Zevi and Jacob Frank. Interestingly enough, their lives offer less influence on Jewish-American poetry than the three preceding movements. There have been a substantial number of novels written about these historical characters, for the most part rather straightforward historical novels, indicating not specially imaginative transformations of fictive narration.⁴³ We must conclude that some elements in these two movements seem less attractive to the poetic mind than the elements found in the other manifestations of apocalyptic messianism. Most characteristic of Shabbatianism and Frankism is the great literalness of the lives of the two messianic aspirants. Their thoughts and their theories are almost entirely derivative from the Lurianic *kabbalah*. Only their actions are distinctive. Since one of the great shared concerns of this poetry is the concern with speech and expression, not fact, the lives of Shabbatai Zevi and Jacob Frank do not offer the same richness in linguistic experimentation that the other sources do.

The seventeenth-century Shabbatai Zevi and the eighteenth-century Jacob Frank were followers of the ancient Jewish traditions of messianism, as well as more recent theories stemming from the sixteenth-century Lurianic school of *kabbalah*. In the most extreme expressions, the followers of these two men came to an almost nihilistic, or at least antinomian, response to the laws of Torah. The popular twentieth-century Jewish view rejects these men and their movements as anti-Jewish and self-destructive aberrations, merely Jewish responses to the anti-Semitism of Europe. The Jewish-American poets refer to both the historically accurate traditional placement of these messiahs and to the popular Jewish fear and misconceptions of the movements.

The two movements, Shabbatianism and Frankism, were intimately related historically. Shabbatai Zevi (1626–1676), born in Smyrna, was a man of great personal charm and beauty, who suffered from what today would most likely be termed manic-depression,[44] but viewed quite differently by his followers. The manic states were states of illumination during which he performed all sorts of questionable rituals including a marriage ceremony and dance with a Torah scroll and his most shocking act of anti-nomianism—conversion to Islam. The depressions marked times in which God turned away His face from His Messiah. As important to the movement as Shabbatai Zevi, Nathan of Gaza, his prophet, functioned much as Elijah, to announce the coming of Messiah and to explain all of Shabbatai Zevi's peculiar behavior. Nathan even satisfied many Jews about the apostasy, by describing it as a required fall into the realm of evil in order to return the sparks of creation to the original stasis. Nathan's writings on his leader seem peculiar, but they are quite in keeping with the Jewish apocalyptic. However, many of the followers of the movement, after Nathan's death, were not as circumspect as Nathan. The most outlandish example of nontraditional response to Shabbatianism was by an early eighteenth-century prophet, Baruchiah Russo, whose movement was centered in Salonika.

Baruchiah was a direct influence on Jacob Frank. Frank (1726–1791) perceived himself as the third incarnation of the Messiah—Shabbatai Zevi being the first, Baruchiah the second. The Frankish tendencies toward nihilistic theology and perverted sexual practice as expressions of the new Torah have become legendary in Jewish history. In fact, much of the discomfort with the Shabbatian heresy in Jewish history is in reality disgust with the Frankists and a tendency to attribute all the excesses of the latter movement to its predecessor.

Some of the contemporary translations of Shabbatian and Frankist sources reveal a difference between the two movements. The fullest Frankist excerpts available in English, translated by Harris Lenowitz, are nihilistic in temperament.[45] In them, female sexuality is a temptation rarely resisted and the female principle becomes a powerful goddess of pagan or Marianic influence. She is no longer the female aspect of God, *Shekinah*. She is the Virgin, lover, queen, redeemer, and savior. On the other hand, texts attributed to Shabbatai Zevi and translated by Jack Hirschman, Harris Lenowitz, and Jerome Rothenberg, though antinomian in nature reveal a mystical concern with telling the history of Messiah and with the redemption of the followers.[46] For his followers, the Commandments of Zevi became simply more contemporary versions of the ancient laws of Judaism.

These men and their movements, the most literal and decadent of Jewish apocalyptic messianism, have influenced Jewish-American poetry variously. For the most part, they inspired moralistic teatises on the danger of anarchy. In all their appearances, these Jewish messianic movements seemed to coincide with a great struggle for the Jewish people. Surely the destruction of the European Jews by the most enlightened of Christian European countries would count as a parallel to the loss of the Temple, the explusion of the Jews from Spain in 1492, and the Chmelnicki pogroms. The Holocaust, particularly surprising after the promises of assimilation in *Haskalah*, becomes a historical manifestation of the birthpangs of the Messiah in the apocalyptic tale of the Messiah. But the great shock of the Holocaust makes it impossible for many American Jews and most Gentiles to accept the fullness of its horror. According to some of the most active contemporary Jewish theologians, not until after 1966 did Jewish theology attempt to confront the theological questions raised by these persecutions. This denial was even more apparent in the literature and theology of those Jews who lived in America, a country that was protected from the more grisly aspects of that war. But even America could not deny the pictures of the living skeletons peering through the fences at Auschwitz. By 1961, a major American film studio had transformed a 1950s *Playhouse 90* script into the big budget film *Judgment at Nuremberg*; by 1980, a major southern novelist, scion of Faulknerian family trees, William

Styron, had written a novel of his own naive introduction to the Holocaust through a survivor of Auschwitz. In the Jewish-American consciousness, the sense of the Holocaust has been continuous since the 1940s. But explicit statements do not appear significantly in the literature until the 1960s.[47] The apocalyptic tendency associated with the chaos and threatened anti-Semitism of the Holocaust is thus not surprising to be found in the Jewish-American writer. Further, the celebration of the word, the attention even to letter values, so typical of apocalyptic writing, is particularly attractive to these contemporary poets.

Chapter 2

Apocalyptic Historiography And The Messianic Hopeful

The apocalyptic historiography of the poetry discussed in this book must be placed within the context of the work of some of the most creative historians of the modern period. This theory of history depends on a contemporary interpretation of the Holocaust. For instance, the literary critic, theologian, and historian, Walter Benjamin, has referred to a "messianic standing still" of events, indicating the sense of stasis associated with the messianic evaluation of history.[1] Most theories of the impact of the Holocaust on the twentieth century call it the seminal event of this century, one that in Benjamin's terms causes time to stop, for it transforms our understanding of man and God, and makes us reevaluate what preceded that event and perceive differently what came after that event. Even more influential in the understanding of contemporary apocalyptic historiography is the great reinterpreter of Jewish history, Gershom Scholem.

Scholem does not write of the Holocaust per se, rather of the reinterpretation of the apocalyptic and mystical antinomianism, which delineates the philosophy of most of the false messiahs from the Middle Ages to the present. Born of an assimilated Jewish family of Berlin, Scholem, more than any other man in the twentieth century has changed our ideas about Jewish history and peoplehood. In direct opposition to his heritage and to most historians of Judaism, Scholem spent his life in the study of *kabbalah*, apocalyptic

literature, and false messiahs. Rather than arguing for the ra-
tionalization of messianism, Scholem maintains that this significant
Jewish doctrine was always associated with catastrophe and revolution.[2] Therefore, the apocalyptic expectation of the Messiah presup-
poses a hope for the end of time, an end to history. For Scholem,
this break with the present implies a belief in a new law, a new
Torah. He sees the apocalyptic sense in the tradition of *kabbalah*
from Merkabeh to the Lurianic preparation for the antinomianism of
Shabbatai Zevi. According to Scholem, the moving forces in history
are the demonic and the destructive. A history moves not by logical
development but by surprising contrasts and negations.[3] Messianism, itself a contradiction, an impossibility, expresses *"life lived
in deferment,"* for when the messianic life is explicit, Scholem writes
"then it is foolishly decried (or one might say, unmasked) as pseudo-
Messianism." This contradiction makes of Jewish messianism "the
real anti-existentialism idea."[4] Scholem's counter-history, then,
balances exoteric and esoteric traditions, with the esoteric, the hidden, often negating the exoteric and indeed directing true history.[5]

    References in recent Jewish-American poetry to specific mes-
sianic hopefuls far outweigh similar references in prose. However,
several recent novels relating the life of a false messiah bear on this
discussion. Their more literal expression of the tales of the Messiah
will help the reader see the significance of the more poetic transformations manifest in the poetry. These pieces of historical fiction
should be placed in the theoretical framework of Georg Lukacs's *The
Historical Novel.* He first articulated the tenuous but essential
balance between accuracy of fact and individual creative interpretation.[6] Historical circumstances, the facts of the event cited, the concrete details, therefore, cannot be thought of in the same fashion as
those same facts, circumstances, or details when they appear in a
historical narrative. The aesthetic function in fiction transforms
them.[7] The individual creative mind interacts with subject matter in
all writing, but it does so in a more subjective fashion with any story
of fiction than it does with the biography or the history of a period.
Undoubtedly, there must be some personal identification of the
novelist with the historical era chosen as background for the story.[8]
But the author will express this identification in a variety of man-
ners.

Practitioners of historical fiction have often defended the truth of their narrative by arguing their right to recreate history. One of the most successful of historical fiction writers, Leon Feuchtwanger, writes that in writing historical literature "the creative writers desire only to treat contemporary matters even in those of their creations which have history as their subject. . . . Such writers want only to discuss their relation to their own time, their own personal experiences and how much of the past has continued into the present."[9] A similar impulse permeates the work of these Jewish-American writers, both poets and novelists, who write of the messiahs of the medieval period. They really wish to express their apocalyptic feelings about twentieth-century America. A characteristic of the apocalyptic genre itself, the hidden agenda of the present clothed in the garb of the past, makes for powerful literature.

Some contemporary Jewish-American poets and novelists seem less concerned with the particulars of apocalyptic messianism and more concerned with the fact of its existence, and its relationship to other traditions in Judaism. For instance, in "The Apocalypse is a School for Prophets," Irving Feldman inverts the conventional argument about the historical and theological relationship of the tradition of prophecy to the tradition of apocalypse. Historically, the books of prophecy predate apocalyptic literature. But Feldman maintains that the prophetic temper grows out of apocalyptic visions and characters; cherubim with trumpets and "blazing wind machines" announce prophecy.[10] Only after years of violence and destruction do "scenes from the new life drift[　] over/the blank lustrous curve of their eyes." These prophets are "misanthropic," content to doom mankind to destruction and to celebrate a victory of sorts over ruined wine in a dead beer garden, while mankind suffers destruction. For Feldman, then, an apocalyptic attitude as such is negative, because it is antihuman. Myra Sklarew also chaffs under the requirements of the apocalyptic tradition of messianism. In "Instructions for the Messiah," she writes

> do you think
> you must work signs
> and miracles
> or resurrect the dead.[11]

For her it would be sufficient merely to have read Torah, to have studied *Halakah*. Unlike the Christian tradition of Messiah, Jewish messianism rarely invented dominion for its Messiah. She writes,

> we would ask of you
> only the rebuilding
> of the temple
> and the gathering in
> of the exiles.

Then all of existence would be understandable, reasonable. The messianic magic supported by apocalyptism, for her, seems to be precisely the cause of the Messiah's delay. Unlike Feldman, Sklarew does not accuse apocalyptic of being antihuman, rather of being counterproductive.

An interesting contrast to these poetic renditions is the more fully developed version of the Messiah in Arthur A. Cohen's novel *In the Days of Simon Stern*. Simon, a messianic aspirant born of immigrant parents, secluded in the Jewish downtown until the dispersal of his people after a fire, builds a fortress and temple in the middle of the Lower East Side of New York City. An apparent symbolic re-creation of the history of the Jewish people, the story presents a meditation on the theme of the Messiah, history, and death, and cannot be read as a simple historical novel. Its geographical setting makes it clearly a commentary on Jewish-American dispersal from the Lower East Side, while Simon's innocence about the Gentile world in general, and the European Gentile world in particular, as well as his phenomenal wealth make him a type for the American Jew of the twentieth century. Cohen suggests two actual historical messiahs in the names Simon Stern and Nathan of Gaza. Simon bar Kochba (son of a star) was a military leader called Messiah by Rabbi Akiba (note that "stern" also means "star" in Yiddish). Further, Simon's historian, Nathan, who tells most of the tale, shares the same first name as Shabbatai Zevi's disciple.

In the novel, Cohen shows much interest in analyzing the nature of being a Jew, and of being the most Jewish of Jews, the Messiah. *In the Days of Simon Stern* portrays Jews as sufferers, mourners, pacifists, rememberers, and survivors. They are Jews in everything. As the Last Jew on Earth responds to "How so a Jew?": "I am a Jew in the flesh. I am circumcised. I am a Jew in the spirit. I await the Messiah. I am a Jew by nature and profession. I am patient."[12] This last Jew on earth, an ordinary Jew, in fact, becomes a lesson to the world, a sort of Messiah, just as is Simon. Both are particular expressions of the Messiah, each a "flawed particularity" of the universal form (p. 16). Part of Simon's particularity derives from his Americanness: he is the son of immigrants, he is a capitalist, he is eclectic in his reading, and he is quite practical. The language of the novel expresses the duality of Jewish-American messiahship. From the beginning, Nathan, the narrator, does not know what to call himself, because English does not have an appropriate term for his position:

> The English language is helpless before such requirements and I write all this in English. Simon required English of us, believing it the second language of the world, the language of exchange and intercourse, carnal union, embracing everyone finally. Hebrew he reserved for his testaments, for his chapters of the history of the universe, for prayer and thought; but it's in English, he said, that the world heaves and groans. English: language of the fallen angels. Hebrew: language of anticipation, honey in dew, tongue of new beginnings and salvation (p. 2).

Not only the expression of things in language, but also the Jew's very existence becomes dual, as in the case of Simon who is learned yet practical, small yet powerful, spiritual yet greedy for money. Written in English and set in New York, Nathan's book becomes a specifically American version of Holocaust and Messiah.

Though American Jews did not suffer in concentration camps, Cohen suggests that they survived the Holocaust experience. They must assume the responsibility of survivorship. Cohen also parallels Stern's protective compound with the state of Israel in 1948. As Stern financed the compound, American Jews helped finance the new state. Janos Baltar, the force of death, violence, and deception, housed at first in the new compound, causes the eventual destruction of the New Temple, the new state. The flight of the people out into the city in the novel and the movement of Simon uptown further indicates that Cohen does not see the secular state of Israel as the reestablishment of Eretz Yisroel. For Cohen, Jewish contemporary life continues in *goles* whether it be in New York City or Tel Aviv. The Jewish messianic history for Arthur Cohen becomes a means of commenting on contemporary Jewish existence. The Messiah's physical presence is less significant than his moral presence. But unlike the poems by Irving Feldman and Myra Sklarew, Cohen's Messiah remains very much a human. Simon Stern is in and of this world, his experience is ours. Sklarew and Feldman in their responses on the literal level to the Messiah figure react to a sort of force outside man's power, an unhuman happening that results in unhuman consequences.

The Jewish Messiah story, however, often describes him in thoroughly physical terms, as an exceptionally handsome man. The Shabbatian legend emphasized that element of physical feature and sexual attraction most emphatically. In Rose Drachler's "Athens and Jerusalem," the Messiah as contemporary handsome star is the central feature of a contrast between Jewish and Greek (that is, Western non-Jewish) culture. Her poem begins by describing the geographic beauty of the Greek islands, seas, and skies. But the difference between this ancient land and another is early noted:

> . . . The air here was
> good as in Jerusalem, dry smelling of
> grey rosemary and thyme, but it did not tremble.
> The gold light was quiet and calmly still.[13]

The females of Greece "measured/light of the old, culpable gods" and described their own dress as reasonable and plain. They live in "dry, clear air of [their] past." Their gods, almost as fallible as man, reach backward in time; their women, comfortable in "plain woolens," seem separate from any divine promise or threat.

However, in Jerusalem, the air "trembles." The street resounds with bus traffic, Persian rugs hang from balconies, and "pudding-breasted houris/from Marrakesh" lean out windows. The Messiah, unlike the Greek gods, is imminent in Jerusalem:

. . . Here in the light that
is much more than light, in the
singing sweetness of golden
motes, in the honeyed breath of
the Shechina, the Messiah
will wear an Italian silk
suit cut in the latest mode
and drive a fine, white sports car (p. 118).

Drachler identifies Israel with the *kabbalistic* female principle of God (*Shekinah*), who welcomes her lover with honey sweet breath and song. His advent on the Jerusalem street will call all the "curly wives" onto the balconies to see "the Man as beautiful/as the latest movie star." Drachler's Messiah echoes not the ascetic Christian tradition of Jesus but the physical splendor of what we have come to call a Greek God, who comes to Jerusalem not Athens. Further, the Semitic women not the Greek ones come openly to their windows to exclaim at his beauty. For Ms. Drachler, the Jewish Messiah and the Jewish tradition derive their eternal power from the open sexual attraction of male and female.

The legendary power of Drachler's Messiah quite literally inspires through sexual powers. But not all who see these powers will recognize them as messianic nor interpret them in the same fashion. Edouard Roditi's "The Messiah Ben Joseph" suggests at least four varieties of response to Messiah. The father in the poem begins, in a traditional fashion, reading from a book. His interpretation is:

The written word foretells that he
Must fulfill all prophecies, transmute
Our world-old dream that hounds us through
The hostile years with hope of peace.[14]

His son's violent reaction provides more evidence that the Messiah is indeed about to come. In order to effect his Messiah, a socialistic state, the son asks the father to burn books so that the father can see the pain of his fellow man. The son wishes to make a heaven on earth. He is unwilling to await the comfort of the afterlife. Pregnant with Him, the daughter feels an even more physical presence of Messiah, and the mother looks on in confusion as her son "bears a timeless anguished look" and her daughter "a new/Unknown spring of joy" (p. 26). The poem indicates the wonder and fear that greet a new age. The family members represent all the different attitudes toward such change: the father, only able to see a change if the past has predicted it; the son, desirous of change whether it be progress or not; the daughter, physically feeling that transformation, but incapable of understanding it; and the mother, the one who can see the differences and who knows the violence that must come. Roditi uses the Messiah legend to comment on revolution as a combination of fear and love of progress.

Some pieces of literature by Jewish-American writers go beyond the specifics of the legendary characteristics of the Messiah and instead refer to details of historical appearances of messianic aspirants. There are poems about Abraham Abulafia, a novel about Shlomo Molkho, poems about Isaac Luria, and novels and poems about Shabbatai Zevi and Jacob Frank.

The personage of Abraham Abulafia and his *kabbalah* have been quite influential on the poetry of David Meltzer, Jack Hirschman, and Jerome Rothenberg. Some of the discussion of the influence of Abulafianism on these poets will appear in Chapter 4 under the more theoretical analysis of the influence of the Hebrew alphabet on the ontology of the apocalyptic; however, it is the spectacular life and charismatic personality of the thirteenth-century Abraham Abulafia that affects some of the poems by these authors.

David Meltzer's "Abulafia" in section I of *Yesod* is a case in point. The poem refers to the *kabbalah* of Abulafia, but the man, Abulafia, and his personal impact on his followers forms the center of the poem. As suggested in the song of Yehudi, music assumes superrational significance for David Meltzer, just as it did in Abulafia's *kabbalah*. In his translation of Abulafia's treatise, *Haye Olam Ha-Ba*, Meltzer writes of the proper manipulation of letters that will "create many melodies."[15] For Meltzer, music becomes the metaphor for understanding in his own poetry. In the final section of "Abulafia," he writes,

> Numbers combined & refined
> guide the eye to the one
> the two, the great
> circle where our dance begins.[16]

Numerical manipulation and dance movements indicate the technique by which poetic inspiration is attained. In later stanzas, Meltzer writes

> what do I know now?
> shuttle words & notes
> about, around
> to find a central sound
> the pure tone
> shuffle alphabet (*Yesod*, p. 27).

The sound is the meaning. But unlike Abulafia's mystical search for union with God's reasoning, Meltzer's aim is to understand the role of poet.

Meltzer begins the poem by calling on the spirit of Abulafia, as source of his Jewish mystical inspiration. Writing of "our art," he describes it as "silent queer weirdness/offering all words, all song," an allusion to the Talmudic distrust of representational art (*Yesod*, p. 23). His Abulafia keeps hiding in the poem, surprising the poet as that poet watches television and even as he writes the poem. In section five, Meltzer likens Abulafia's historical Papal visit to a "Niagara" of poems, a drowning in inspiration. Thereby, Abulafia's actions are concrete poems. Meltzer finds in Abulafia's art a pure, nonrational, aesthetic, which indicates true creativity and freedom. Learning the techniques of meditation, Meltzer often quotes Abraham Abulafia in the last two sections of his poem. "Untie the knots, unseal the soul," Meltzer writes as a description of his inspirational techniques (*Yesod*, p. 26). Abraham Abulafia, in his unpublished manuscripts, often repeats the phrase "to unseal the soul, to untie the knots which bind it,"[17] as a description of his aim in *kabbalah*. Meltzer refers to "7 Steps in the Mystic Ladder," a direct reference to Abulafia's seven steps to the summit of mystical and prophetic understanding of godhead (*Yesod*, p. 26). "[S]ekhel, maskil, muskal/*Knowledge, Knower, Known" in Meltzer's "Abulafia" (*Yesod*, p. 26) echoes a fragment from the unpublished piece by Abulafia, *The Knowledge of the Messiah and the Redeemer*:

> And just as his Master, who is detached from all matter, is called

Sekhel, Maskil and *Muskal,* that is the *knowledge,* the *knower* and the *known,* all at the same time, since all three are one in Him, so also he, the exalted man, the master of the exalted name, is called *intellect,* while he is actually knowing; then he is also *the known,* like his Master; and then there is no difference between them, except that his Master has his supreme rank by His own right and not derived from other creatures, while he is elevated to his rank by the intermediary of creatures.[18]

Meltzer's union of poet, poem, and inspiration parallels Abulafia's unity of poet, mentor, and idea. Meltzer ends the poem: *"dillug & kefitsah/*jumping & skipping," the very words used by Abulafia to describe the meditative goal of his *kabbalah (Yesod,* p. 27).

Jack Hirschman's explicit Abulafian reference can be found in two poems included in his collection *Black Alephs.* "Eluardian Elohenu for Allen Ginsberg" describes Ginsberg as a prophet of America's conscience:

Allen first gut and guru of the fall
out to innocent streetboy terror and
nightly chants of syllables abulafian.[19]

In his contradictions, Ginsberg represents the Abulafian prophet for Hirschman, an exilic poet with "dangerous innocence" who combined the eastern chant with the western rhythms. As is true of most of Hirschman's poems written during the sixties and early seventies, the spectre of the Viet Nam War looms even in this poem of faint praise for a mentor.

Hirschman's "Hymn" also paints an image of a prophet and the disciple's perception of that mentor.[20] However, this mentor transforms himself into the follower as well as into the Messiah, just as the prophet of Abulafian *kabbalah* transforms himself into the viewer. The disciple in Hirschman's poem must become small, "dropping everything/becoming Zero" in order to attain *kabbalistic* spiritualization. The meditator then sees Abraham and Isaac, speaks with an "aaronic mouth," that is a priestly (thereby more lowly than prophetic) mouth. In his priestly guise, the disciple "needs things to hold to/objects calves imaginary." He is not meditating on the abstraction of abstractions like Moses "who needs/Nothing." Only when he approaches the book of Raziel Ha-Melech (Raziel, the Angel) with the love of a mother for a child does he feel the "breath of the/letters pouring/into me." Significantly Hirschman chooses Raziel as the angelic communicator in this passage, for Abraham Abulafia chose Raziel as a pseudonym for himself. The hymn to himself, as his own angelic mentor, ends with a direct reference to the proper meditative technique according to Abraham Abulafia. In his manuals on meditation, Abulafia describes layers of meditation when studying the letters: articulation, *mivta*, writing, *miktav*, thought, *mahshav*. In Jack Hirschman's "Hymn," the final two stanzas describe that very same layering:

<blockquote>

by mivta by
    miktav by mahshav
       for nothing ever is lost
by mahshav by miktav by mivta
    everything upheld
   every smell of deep
    earth as a child
       every white mittyblouse
every street
    seen by mivta pain
     tasted by miktav every
   knee laceration youth incarnation spat
    arm pit old smells crying
     done dead or aborted
      by mahshav
       upheld.

</blockquote>

Jerome Rothenberg often refers to Abulafia in his poetry. Sometimes he merely quotes texts as in "History Seven" which begins with a quotation from *Sha'erei Zedek*, by one of Abulafia's disciples, describing the student's response to the seventy-two names of God.[21] But in his long poem *Abulafia's Circles*, Rothenberg structures an entire poem on some of the biographical features of Abraham Abulafia as well as on some of the spiritual aspects of the relationship between disciple and leader. The first section of the three-part poem is entitled "Abulafia." The other two sections are of

Jacob Frank and Tristan Tzara, who here become reincarnations of Abulafian messiahship. The structure then suggests the same posi-tion of influence and inspiration for the Abulafia figure that Hirschman and Meltzer gave him. However, the poem is even more significantly controlled by the Abulafian *kabbalah* than by the man Abraham Abulafia and it responds more to ontological than to sociological/aesthetic questions. Therefore, most of the discussion of it will be deferred to Chapter 4.

Another messianic aspirant who has appeared in contemporary Jewish-American literature is Shlomo Molkho. Harry Simonhoff, in *The Chosen One*, a traditional historical novel, relates the tale of the sixteenth-century messianic movement in Europe which centered on the two figures of Shlomo Molkho and David Reubeni. Mr. Simonhoff intends to provide, within the context of the few historical facts, a personal, psychological, and spiritual portrait of the character of Shlomo Molkho, born a Marrano in Portugal. Molkho's gradual appearance in the public eye as messianic aspirant, his studies in Safed, his trip to Rome to confer with the Pope, and his eventual burning at the stake at an auto-da-fé are matters of history. But his personal relationships to the hierarchy of the Church, the members of the Illuminati of sixteenth-century Italy, and his lover of the demimonde are not. The additional details suggest to the reader possible explanations for the messianic hopes of Molkho. Diego Pirez, a Christian scribe who works at the court of Portugal's king, becomes Shlomo Molkho, a Jewish saint, who spends his time in prison speculating on the *kabbalistic* significance of numerical manipulations of the seventy-two letter name of God. Born into a house decorated with crosses and with portraits of Mary and Jesus, he dies shouting the *Shema*. His metamorphosis, though more exag-gerated, follows a pattern of a notable portion of American Jews from assimilationist to militantly Jewish.

Simonhoff transforms this individual history into a symbol of Jewish martyrdom. At the end, Molkho's individual sacrifice sym-bolizes all Jewish sacrifice, *Kiddush ha-Shem*, in the face of Gentile bigotry. After Molkho's awesome scream and prayer, Simonhoff concludes

And so the obsolete and archaic long banished in religion periodically returns. Horror and bloodshed had their mysterious appeal to primitive man. In his deep subconscious the human breast has never forgotten the thrilling pain, the unendurable attraction of human sacrifice. Once again a son of Israel chosen for the role of martyr was ready, yea eager, to become a blood *Korban* for *Kiddush Hashem*.[22]

For Simonhoff, Molkho becomes the ransom for all, indeed the act of the Jewish Messiah. The author uses Molkho's story to illustrate just how the martyr can function as saint, how an individual can be trapped into an historical necessity that requires his own destruction. By knowing the final outcome, Simonhoff maintains, we can understand the past. Like the Messiah of Cohen's novel, Simonhoff's Molkho seems a believable human being. But Simonhoff's interpretation of the messianic life and his parallel to martyrdom is simplistic. The questions of moral responsibility and supernatural power raised by the Jewish idea of Messiah can not best be developed in a novel that is primarily a realistic historical novel.

Jack Hirschman has written two poems that allude to the power of another messianic figure, Isaac Luria, the Ari.[23] The shorter of the poems, "The R of the Ari's Raziel," is a meditation on the fate of Jacqueline Bouvier Kennedy Onassis. "The Ari," the more significant poem, on the other hand, not only uses the historical features of contemporary America to comment on human relations and the apocalypse, but also turns to Jewish mystical theories, and therefore will be discussed in Chapter 3. In both, however, the central energy is the male lion, Ari.

The narrator of "The R of the Ari's Raziel" remembers the death of John Kennedy:

eight years to the night the street
lights lowered like lips on the nod
the length of the fixed arm of an
idea jammed with the point of the world's
bullet rushing to the brain . . . .

as he sees the new Mrs. Onassis. The world looks at a changed Jacqueline, with her "eyes once vogue/of princesses . . . hidden by
shades," and beside her stands the spectre of the crude Ari: "her
mouth the lips of Athens/jammed with a cigar." As the poet maintains the perspective of the public, he echoes the desire to dig up the
myth of Kennedy in order to cruelly "Prop him up in the chair with a
strawhat." But he remembers the death and the "embers
dismembered/in the November blood." This final star and fire image
reminds the reader of the spewing brain matter of the Kennedy
assassination as well as the fire's suggestion of hope. The name
"Raziel" adds to the impact of the poem, for Raziel was the angelic
inspiration of Abraham Abulafia as well as his choice for pseudonym
in the apocalyptic. In similar fashion, Jacqueline assumes the role of
angel or apostle/inspiration for Aristotle Onassis and for John F.
Kennedy. As Ari's Raziel she is successful, but as Kennedy's she is
not. Hirschman ends with a grotesque image of the female
character. After propping up the corpse of Kennedy, giving a
cigarette and drink to him,

> the Jacqueline
> puffs throws back her head throws out her groin
> gives up a placenta of childless fiery points
> washing the wounds of revolution in old flames'
> black rabbits out of the man's high silk hat.

The fire she produces is infertile; her magic is from the old man's
silk hat, from the Onassis money. This Ari does not have Isaac
Luria's spiritual money, nor even John F. Kennedy's honorable
leadership, he has simply the power of the moneyed elite of the contemporary world. His very crude physicality contrasts to the
spiritual presence of Luria.

    In this poem, Hirschman combines his pacifist philosophy with
his admiration of the Camelot of John F. Kennedy's administration.
He turns from despair only through the transmutation of *kabbalistic*
literary history. Luria's theory of creation out of destruction is particularly important to Hirschman's constructed optimism as is
Luria's image of the goddesslike qualities of *Shekinah*. But most im-

portant in this poem is the powerful presence of Isaac Luria himself. Though he produced little literary output himself, he transformed the *kabbalistic* landscape and Jewish history; the Ari is a powerful guru of the Jewish contemporary mystic. He magically transforms angels, as the Svengali-like Aristotle Onassis did to America's First Lady. But Ari transforms for the good of the people, whereas Onassis for completely selfish purposes.

In translations of actual Shabbatian poems, contemporary poets have indicated some of their greatest debts to the leading figure of that messianic movement. For instance, Jack Hirschman's translation of Jacob Tausk of Prague's "Ein Schon Neu Lied fun Moschiach," tells the history of Shabbatai Zevi's messiahship.[24] Tausk promises salvation even after Zevi's apostasy:

> the Turks threw him into prison
> but as soon as he entered
> the light glowed,
> the four walls began to burn all around, red as fire.
> Men in prison with him beheld the glow.
> The Turks then wanted to set him free immediately
> but our King would not leave the jail (p. 226).

From the believer's perspective, Zevi's actions become resistance and bravery. Jerome Rothenberg also has translated several Ladino lyrics in the Shabbatian tradition, most of which praise Shabbatai Zevi as Messiah.[25] He is the "glow of true messiah," the serpent who gave the Jews freedom, "myrrh root," of Jesse's root:

> the fourth leg of the chariot
> went down into the sea
> fought Samael.

He is opposer of Satan. These lyrics indicate a respectable and indeed attractive attitude toward Zevi. His charisma and personal beauty seem to communicate themselves through the three centuries and several languages into our day. These translations are indeed contemporary evaluations of a man of tremendous personal charm, but questionable character. His presence can be felt in several examples of poetry and prose of the recent period. Of the several novels by American Jews about Shabbatai Zevi, the most recent, Leonard Wolf's *The False Messiah*, is one of the best. A highly sexual rendition of the life of this messianic hopeful, *The False Messiah* depends very little on objective narration. A series of accounts from multiple narrators portrays Shabbatai Zevi. The reader never sees him without a filter. These filters include his various followers: Peter Harleigh, a Christian homosexual who loves him physically; Nehemiah ha-Kohen, Jewish survivor of pogroms who questions his messiahship; Nathan of Gaza, his major spokesman; Sarah, his whorish wife; and Barot'ali, an idiot, but his first disciple. Toward the end of the novel, Peter writes: "In my darkest moments, I charge Shabbatai with having been an empty space filled by the longing of those who loved, and thereby invented, him. Then I remember his eyes, the touch of his hand, his smell, and the radiance of his smile, and I am baffled once more."[26] In fact, Peter is right; Wolf suggests that Shabbatai was a product of others minds. Our contemporary sense of the historical figure of Shabbatai Zevi represents a combination of portraits and judgments by followers, critics, and students of Shabbatai Zevi. In fact, Wolf's portrait of Shabbatai Zevi benefits greatly from Gershom Scholem's masterful 1973 biography of Zevi, a psychological portrait of a manic-depressive, led and molded by others.

The fact that Shabbatai Zevi's earliest disciple was an idiot is particularly poignant and revealing. Despite physical mistreatment, Barot'ali loves his master with the complete abandon of the mentally incompetent. The idiot's vision ends the novel, and a despairing vision it is. Barot'ali, crowing as a rooster to help the sun to rise every morning, mourns, for "what rises is always the wrong sun" (p. 278). His idiot's despair echoes a similar disappointment in all of Zevi's followers. Speculating earlier on the history of Shabbatai's rise of power, Nehemiah had wondered "Was it madness born of grief? Or was it a sign of hope? Madness and hope! What was Jewish history if not a single rope braided of those two strands?" (p. 219). Nehemiah puts words on the tension in Jewish history between chaos and order, insanity and rationality. Wolf's composite portrait of Shabbatai Zevi indicates this tension most clearly; it is his own evaluation of apocalyptic historiography. Like Cohen, Wolf uses the novel form to make a theoretical statement beyond the significance of one human's life. However, his fiction does not touch on the moral realm, the thematic realm of most poetry based on Shabbatai Zevi.

John Hollander's "The Loss of Smyrna" makes Shabbatai Zevi's character the basis for a stringent criticism of contemporary society. Hollander writes a dream vision of a return to Smyrna, the hometown from which Shabbatai Zevi was first expelled for heretical activity some time between 1651 and 1654. He returned in 1665 after he had gained quite a large following as the Messiah. The first three months of his return were quiet ones, probably coinciding with one of his depressive states. In December of that year, the illumination returned to him and thus began a period of intense and ever more frenzied and questionable religious activity. The next year he was arrested by the Turkish authorities. After his apostasy, he never returned home. However, his hometown remained one of the strongholds of his movement and always seemed a place for him of power and inspiration. Hollander begins his poem with the narrator writing of a depressed state, "Sick and weak," remembering better days. The solution only comes to him when he remembers Smyrna: "Port of Venus!" The narrator hires a ship and sails in quite unpleasant conditions to the consolation of this port:

Borne thus bravely over despairing's ocean
By the wild, bright dream of those domes, and reaching
Port at last, I joyed at the end of motion,
        Firmness of beaching.[27]

However, he sees not a dome, but a sandy, flat beach, like a beach on the Gulf of Mexico. At this disappointing sight, the speaker screams, "Oi, Weh! Izmir!"—punning on the Yiddish exclamation and the other name for the town Smyrna (that is, Izmir)—indicating that Izmir, whatever its pretense of beauty and consolation, is really nothing other than pain (p. 95).

A Radcliffe graduate, recently turned whore, leads the narrator to the domes, towers, courts, and gardens that "seem to burn a/Flame within [his] memory still!" (p. 96). Smyrna, no longer merely a mental yearning, becomes a real physical presence surrounding him. Led to the pleasure palaces of Smyrna, he sees opulent colors that embarrass the colors of the rainbow and forbidden sins that make Electra blush: "Circe outdoes herself there." Smyrna represents a place of eternal freedom and frightening license: sodomy, flagellation, and masochism all appear boldly as allowable. But

> Suddenly Night fell—not a night of blisses
> Filled with Smyrning raptures—but reedy fluting,
>   Turning to hisses,
>
> Surged behind my temples and—blink and swallow—
> There I lay. Cold Winter had just uncrowned me.
> SMYRNA? Gone! gone in a vision's hollow
>   Smashing around me (pp. 97–98).

Awakened from his dream, the narrator realizes that the other side of license is pain. Hollander criticizes the self-destructiveness of life without traditional bounds. Published in his collection *Spectral Emanations*, this dream vision of the pain of lawlessness becomes, in fact, a condemnation of contemporary licentiousness.

Jerome Rothenberg, a poet who has been influenced by almost all versions of Jewish apocalyptic messianism, has written two poems that refer to the antinomian Frankist and Shabbatian movements. "Satan in Goray: A homage to Isaac Bashevis Singer" comments on the Shabbatian movement in a response to I. B. Singer's symbolic tale of the chaos in an East European *shtetl* under the power of Shabbatianism. Rothenberg divides his poem into twelve sections, each echoing themes that he found in Singer's novel: distrust of sects or schisms, the female principle of Shabbatian worship, the Shabbatian physicality alternating with prayer, and Lilith "jest[ing] nudgingly" with Shabbatai Zevi.[28] Further, the poem follows the organization of Singer's novel. However, Rothenberg not only writes a tribute to Singer, he also makes a comment of his own. The juxtaposition of themes from the novel and facts from Shabbatai Zevi's life indicate Rothenberg's idea that man's history is a constant struggle of opposing forces. His vision of Shabbatian excess is less a matter of misplaced dedicaton or madness (Singer's points) than it is a matter of excess of dedication. The second section of Rothenberg's poem *Abulafia's Circles* presents the life and character of Jacob Frank as a return of the Abulafian Messiah. Here, as in the Shabbatian poem discussed above, Rothenberg does not overlook the antinomianism of the movements. However, he sees this antinomianism not as sinful or frightul as does John Hollander in "Loss of Smyrna." In contrast, Hollander's traditionalism, his comfort in structure, most clearly conflicts with Rothenberg's radicalism and comfort in open-ended forms. The two extremes in contemporary Jewish-American poetry found inspiration in the same sources, but offered opposing conclusions.

In the contemporary poetic references to these historical characters and their messianic movements, the facts of these men's lives and their impacts on the Judaism of their days are seminal, but the poets also comment on contemporary society and the failure of moral righteousness in the twentieth century. Of the novelists, Arthur Cohen comes closest to this poetic parallel of messianic lives and didactic comment. His novel is the most poetic in style and structure of the three pieces of fiction discussed in the chapter, and his choice of a Messiah created from multiple historical sources rather than an individual historical Messiah allows him a broader range of themes. In a way similar to all renditions of the messianic legend in Jewish tradition, the original poems and novels that allude to Shabbatai Zevi, Abraham Abulafia, Shlomo Molkho, Isaac Luria, and Jacob Frank depend on both the idiosyncratic details of the men's lives and the general characteristics of messianic legend that they share. The poems and novel discussed in this chapter that do not cite one of these specific messianic aspirants still seem to draw strength from specific historical manifestations of millenarian fervor. In all cases, the authors write with a literal mindedness that will not be found in much of the rest of the literature to be discussed in this book. In these pieces, questions of contemporary morality and the nature of messiahship join together to form a basis for an apocalyptic historiography: everything and everyone are explained by that future event that will end all time.

Chapter 3

Allegory And The Messianic Story

The literal influence of apocalyptic messianism on Jewish-American poetry, as described in the previous chapter, often appears as a specific reference to a particular messianic aspirant or to a particular characteristic of that messianic aspirant. However, the more abstract influences of the apocalyptic on contemporary poetry appear in references to types, to representatives, to symbolic characters, and to representative time frames. In this chapter, the poets discussed will be referring to typological manifestations in the messianic history. Actors in the messianic drama (prophet, angel, demon, *Shekinah*, Lilith) and events in the messianic history (*shevirah ha-Kelim*, epochs of history, messianic birth pangs) symbolize man in relationship to the Messiah, and history in relation to the apocalypse.

The human role closest to the Messiah is, of course, the role of prophet. In general, prophecy can be the result of any direct communication with godhead no matter what the subject. Specifically, in reference to the messianic advent, the prophet is most often identified with Elijah who traditionally announces the Messiah. Rose Drachler's "The Prophet" describes the human potential for prophecy: "He was not born a prophet/He was born able to become one."[1] Particularly apt in sad times, prophecy, after preparation and practice, allows the prophet to follow his dreams and soar above mere mankind. In Drachler's poem "The Witness," the human response to

spiritual/divine happenings is even more mundane, as that witness
stands "foursquare, close to the ground."[2] Harvey Shapiro, in "The
Prophet Announces," writes of Elijah trumpetting the arrival of the
Messiah:

> Elijah with the shofar to his mouth,
> His hand upon the guide reins of the King,
> Who rides an ass. They look so sad.[3]

But only a bird observes the scene, no "New Adam come to greet
the King." In these three poems of human comment on divinity, the
prophet is indeed not respected in his hometown and when he appears as forerunner of the Messiah, he is unsuccessful in his goal. If
prophecy is ineffective, so then must be the Messiah.

A more effective means of divine communication within the
apocalyptic messianic tradition is communication by virtue of
angelic intervention. Irving Feldman writes of angels as messengers
of God in "The Messengers."[4] Only to individuals willing and able to
abandon selfhood do the cherubic creatures in Feldman's poem
speak. These messengers precede the revelation as light precedes
dawn. Howard Schwartz writes of the Jewish sense of the eternity of
angels in "Our Angels." However, for Schwartz, the Jewish angels
are creatures who sleep, who only dream of the reestablishment of
the old order. Nevertheless when they awaken, they will remember
to tend the fire in the eternal flame:

> For them as for us
> There is nothing more beautiful
> Than memory.[5]

Only the recording of history redeems the past and the present.

In the poem *Tohu*, David Meltzer combines his desire for inspiration from a lost Judaic past and his feeling of successful divine
communication as an inspiration for his prophetic poetry.[6] Meltzer
attaches the poem to an epigram from the *Zohar* in which he defines
Tohu as "*a place which has no color and no form. . . . It seems for a moment to have form, but when looked at again it has no form*" (p. 116). For
Meltzer, in this place, the poet achieves his personal inspiration. He

begins the poem with several "Admonitions": "Stay away from these words & all other words," . . . "You dont need a teacher" (p. 116). His advice to the individual poet is observation unencumbered by other human analysis. Only "imagination breaks the code." Meltzer presents an apocalyptic vision of a holocaust that burns Hebrew books, but gives no light, much in keeping with the traditional apocalyptic visions communicated to the prophet by his angelic interlocutor. In Meltzer's words, the prophet leans toward heaven and learns that *"The soul unites with the divine soul in a Kiss"* (p. 118). Meltzer's state after vision and his difficulty in communicating his vision to other human beings follows the traditional apocalyptic mode:

> Vision over, done with.
> 12 angel band together
> & hose the fire off my skull.
> Vision smoke
> pulled back into space,
> into worlds behind worlds
> within the rings I work my art thru (pp. 118–119).

As he tries to tell in the poem, he produces his own obstacles. A storm causes a literal power failure which coincides with the power failure in the poet's creative process: "Right in the middle of writing a poem" (for he does not know touch typing). He must stop his creativity because of his own rational inadequacies, not because the poem, the sign, does not continue.

When the power comes on again, the telephone interrupts Meltzer again and his communication to the unhearing caller provides the center of the poem. Meltzer tells the caller that as a poet he turns to the inspiration of the angels "who hint at it in black words printed on old paper gold-edged by time." He strives to be an apocalyptic initiate, calculator of the messianic advent. Struggling to understand the divine language of creation, he must begin by wrestling with himself and loneliness. While attempting to communicate all of himself, he recognizes that all of himself is not enough. He becomes a dreamer, "new-born shaman," the object of his own contemplation. Nature flows through him, and his davening evokes cries that frighten children. When he turns from man's word (books) to God's word (nature), he assumes the true prophetic stance. In the ascension to prophecy, however, Meltzer recognizes not only the awesome beauty, but also the awesome terror:

> Tell them there are moments when it's all perfect
> above & below, it's perfect
> where sparks in space
> (terrible, beautiful sparks in space)
> are merely metaphors for the world between
> one pore & another (p. 123).

The final section of the poem borrows more from American Indian animism than from Judaism, but it continues the plea for inspiration from powers beyond the individual human. Meltzer admits to being shaman-like. He returns to caves to meditate and to commune with the forces of animal heaven. In this retreat, perhaps meant to mimic the Messiah's retreat into Bird's Nest, the poet "deciphers light songs sung by/the farthest star, the nearest spark." He reads all natural acts, understands the value of all letters and numbers. And from the earth he makes a request:

> *O let earth & all earth's critters know*
> *I was here & I am her's* [sic] *too*
> *Make use of me, sweet Mystery*
> *Make use of me from toe to lotus!* (p. 124).

When such inspiration happens, the poet has been singing with angels, and his singing results in poetry in the most ancient of senses. It is prophecy.

Human sexual union, as a symbol of cosmic union, often appears in mysticism and the Lurianic *kabbalah* is replete with its usage. Such creativity and passion in this context express health. Therefore, the exile of the female principle threatens a dangerous disruption to the right order of things. The mere suggestion of a female principle of God in Judaism is tantamount to heresy, a suggestion some say smacks of Christian Marianic temptation. But careful survey of the Jewish medieval mystical tradition indicates clear female emanations of divinity and some scholars suggest that the tendency stems from even earlier times. In his *The Hebrew God-*

dess, Raphael Patai argues that the *Shekinah* played a part in the prebiblical Jewish consciousness. Legend had it, even before the Lurianic development, that she had lived on earth before the fall and she had exiled herself further and further from earth as biblical man sinned more and more.[7] Another interpretation of the feminine principle's relationship to exiled mankind places responsibility for her exile on the Jewish people. She is exiled because of Israel's sins, in that she goes into exile with the Jews, manifesting herself in nature.[8] In either version, her exile is intimately tied to the exile of Israel. Thus, *Shekinah*, in contemporary Jewish-American poetry, often symbolizes spiritual wholeness and inspiration.

Divided into ten sections, Jack Hirschman's "Ari" purports to be alphabet grams, that is, messages, hieroglyphs, to contemporary readers, in which a female principle provides solace for mankind and overcomes mortality.[9] The ten letters are the first ten letters of the Hebrew alphabet. As indicated in the "Alephgram," the United States determines the perspective but world destruction determines the concern. In the contemporary world, a new unity is apparent, but that unity is based on fear; it is not the unity of *Shekinah* with godhead. Not sure to whom he speaks, the poet suggests the poem is his last cry to a world about to be destroyed. Here love and murder are said in the same breath and the Babylonian exile returns with all its decadence. Hirschman sees contemporary violence as a consequence of the Holocaust and he sees this violence as a murdering of all good, all mystical hope. But in "Dalethgram," Hirschman argues that if we remember the "permutations" of Abulafia three centuries later (which would place the speaker in Luria's century) and in Safed (which would place him in Luria's town), then the violence of time could be healed. In "Dalethgram," Hirschman pulls the reader into the twentieth century:

> Kindly tell the future combinations be kind
> Lay the flames out neatly after much deranging
> Uterine births are necessary up to the point
> Remember the Aleph as you go soaringly down
> Into the moon craters of the daily news finding
> At the source the first rung loveliness of time (p. 119).

Images of destroyed cities and destroyed men abound in this poem; particular deaths of leaders (for example, John F. Kennedy) provide specifics that fit in any time frame, but general death and destruction permeate all places and all time. Hirschman creates a female person "Thou" that can resist death. She can resist even Zyklon, for she is lighter than death and much wiser. But she does not represent denial of past horrors, in fact

> . . . she is least conscious of
> Remembering to forget herself being the remembering
> Indefatiguably remembered in the flesh of flashed
> Apocalypse called the daily bread she turns into (p. 120).

She is *Shekinah*, not to be confused with movie goddesses, or American prom queens. Only *Shekinah* can resist death. And the hero is no Zeus, "He is me simple and plural and genitive" (p. 121). He writes for peace, "the cause of roses," and he writes to "the Queen of this brisk fugitive Jerusalem," the ever elusive kingdom of peace, the Messianic Age (p. 121). Unity with her would not be a unity of fear but of love and life.

Howard Schwartz includes in his collection *Gathering the Sparks* several lyrics that imply that the *Shekinah* has more to do with the accomplishing of *tikkun* (returning the sparks of creation in Lurianic *kabbalah*, therefore attaining salvation) than the male principle of godhead.[10] In "Song of Ascent" and "Neshamah" only a female gathers sparks to return them to the primordial stasis. Schwartz identifies her with a hidden kind of wisdom. In "The Robe of the Shekhina," he associates even her clothing with light. She chooses exile, chooses it in an attempt to comfort those whom she loves:

> She is the one who hovers
> Over the flames
> Of the parchment
> So long
> A spark catches
> The hem of her robe.

After all the letters rise from the parchment, *Shekinah* reforms a robe which in fact "brings the worlds/Closer." In such a manner, she becomes a much more positively active principle in the Lurianic cosmogony than Adonai.

For some contemporary Jewish-American poets, this sexuality of the female becomes the source not only of physical attraction but also of religious inspiration. In "El" by Jack Hirschman, the poet's sexual union with a woman becomes a metaphor for understanding the mysteries of godhead and Talmud. The poem's title, a short-hand reference to Elohim, parallels a human physical encounter with Torah study. Having taken the unnamed woman into a dark room, the poet makes love to her:

> I lay her down her liaison dark and
> not yet black with distance took her
> thighs and spread them wild and wide
> she wrapped me as she had and made
> her whisper as she had him in
> the room was dark but not yet black.[11]

At the moment of climax, the lovers call each other words marking sexual identification, words like "stallion," "cunt," "slut," and "slide." But then, the poet's negative tone changes:

> I broke her into books of dead mishna
> with all the various changes tried
> heaping up broken letters and charred
> bodies of moans and groans and crying
> hatreds grew hills of hair multiplying
> and still out of reach the black fire
> she was in the room beyond her burning.

She has become the people Israel, a commentary (a *mishna*) of Jewishness. The offensive terminology for the female and its shock-ing transformation into positive sexual union indicates the im-possibility of destroying the beauty and power of the female prin-ciple. No matter how degraded the man attempts to make the woman, she will in the end become Torah incarnate. *Shekinah* will be redeemed.

Jack Hirschman uses the sexual relationship as an image for religious appreciation in two other poems. In "The Holy Kabbala," he calls *kabbalistic* study a collection of "rich perversions."[12] The mystical tradition becomes the limit of life, and "She and I are Her." In the union of male and female and of human and nature (that is, "her sister pouring through the window"), the student of *kabbalah* becomes one with the female principle of God in thoroughly sexual unity. In "Zohara," Hirschman's love for Ruth becomes identified with his love and study of the *Zohar*. He describes creation as a female:

> . . . I'm dancing on creation's body   and she is a bookish woman
> who keeps her secret in the leaves   Who is You   Her dark   Her
> green outspreading.[13]

Sometimes the writers elevate the female principle to an aspect of God, *Shekinah*, in Jewish-American poetry. In Edouard Roditi's "Shekhina and the Kiddushim," the idea of *Shekinah* predates the *Yahwehist* in a rather primitive idea of the female.[14] In Jack Hirschman's "There is a Beautiful Maiden Who Has No Eyes Who is the True Messiah," *Shekinah* becomes a Venus figure, rather than a maternal goddess.[15] However, most poets turn to the *Shekinah* as bride of God or container of all that is feminine in nature. For instance Jerome Rothenberg's "She" lists all meanings of *Shekinah*, all ways of female being, all matriarchs of *tanakh*, all names for goddess, and even the negative names for her threatening aspect (such as "stranger," "serpent," "Lilith").[16] As bride, *Shekinah* assumes the most powerful and beautiful of roles. In Rothenberg's "The Bride" in *Poland/1931*, *Shekinah* offers solace to the exiled Jews of Poland. During the pain of the Polish exile, awesome in the images of pogroms and rapes, Rothenberg sees the *Shekinah* as comforting and wise:

> thy tits will I squeeze upon for wisdom
> of a milk that drops like letters
> sacred alphabet soup we lap up . . . .[17]

She protects all Jews in the exile and allows the combination of sexes that will exist in the after life. In fact, then, *Shekinah* attains the position of the final cosmic equater of men, song of angels, and way to America, in Jerome Rothenberg's geographical symbol of release from Europe's persecution of the Jews.

Though the images of *Shekinah* in "The Bride" tend unpleasantly toward the male chauvinistic with such terms as "cunt" and "ass," Rothenberg's *Shekinah* images are not always so. For instance, in a September 1975 entry in his notebooks, writing about Nathaniel Tarn's *Lyrics for the Bride of God*, Rothenberg sees the bride as "smug in the male imagination builds a house for her."[18] Men think they can contain her, but she knows otherwise. She assumes here the position of God, the mother, "who first experienced the *galut* poor old soul." Other Rothenberg uses of *Shekinah* present much more comfortable images of her as a positive sexual creature. For instance, in the long poem *Poland/1931*, two sections refer to the Lurianic concept of *Shekinah*. In these sections, "Galician Nights, or A Novel in Progress" and "Esther K. Comes to America," the poet tells the story of Esther K., a thoroughly human and sexual creature. A mock-up of what could have been an advertisement in a Yiddish newspaper of the 1930s precedes the two sections. A photograph of a Jewish-looking woman in a gypsy-looking scarf accompanies the following text: "You've heard her on the radio, seen her on T.V. now see her in her own home. Mme. Shekinah."[19] Billed as a "Jewish Soul healer and Adviser," she can remove bad luck and bad spirits. In commercial American terms, the *Shekinah* comforts the Jews of the Lower East Side.

The first section provides the background and mysterious past for the woman who tries to serve as American Messiah. However, in the poem "Esther K. Comes to America: 1931," she appears almost powerless. She is exiled from her exile, new in America, in a new wilderness. Her mate, Leo Levy, a self-styled false messiah, in the earlier section meets her again in America: "history repeated itself with marked rapidity."[20] Only her inspiration and her dream can move Leo to his dream of power:

> what lovely dreams the world will have of Esther K.
> said Leo Levy
> I will make dreams for the world to have of Esther K.

& garments to wear in her image
I will comb her hair out until it reaches to Nicaragua
then will climb its length
& let it carry me to the top of a windy boat
sailing for Jerusalem; farewell! (p. 109)

The *Shekinah*, thereby, takes the Messiah home. However, in the end of this story, these two European hopefuls become "an aged couple/smelling of wet sheets." Rothenberg says "the Wilderness/has shrunk them."

Esther and Leo's hopelessness results from the attempt to express this relationship in human physical terms. Esther K. may be a disappointment, but the true *Shekinah* is not, just as the messianic aspirants are disappointments in history, but the Messiah is not. In this same collection, Jerome Rothenberg includes his own version of a Lurianic poem often included in the Jewish liturgy for the Sabbath, " 'Isaac Luria's Hymn to Shekinah for the Feast of the Sabbath' Newly set Rosh Hashonah 5733 by Jerome Rothenberg," as the last entry in "Galician Nights." *Shekinah* and the Bride Sabbath are closely identified in this lyric. The mystic sings of the *Shekinah's* beauty and her fertility and sets a festive table in her honor. As lover he "embraces her/down to foundation."[21] They create new life, new light, and new love. Described as "the bride with/70 crowns" Rothenberg's *Shekinah* follows a traditional image of Lurianic female in-dewlling:

> with her King who
> hovers above her
>
> crown above crown in
> Holy of Holies
>
> this lady all worlds are
> formed in
>
> all's sealed
> within her
>
> shines out from
> Ancient of Days (p. 98).

She is the mate of God and the most valuable jewel in His crown. Credited with giving power to lovers and refuge to all mankind, *Shekinah* overcomes the evil,

the hostile
powers

have left us
demons you feared

sleep in chains (p. 99).

The chains image is of particular significance because usually the Messiah remains in chains until he can return to the earth for the redemption of mankind. But as implied here, during the Sabbath, when the *Shekinah* is present, the Messiah is free, and the forces of evil are bound.

Lilith, the dark side of *Shekinah*, adds a pertinent feature of the symbolic level of apocalyptic influence on Jewish-American poetry. Representing the night and darkness, sexual indiscretion and non-procreative sexual activity, Lilith suggests the feminine force of seduction. But she is also the woman who demanded equality with Adam. These combinations indicate not a simple contrast between good and evil, in *Shekinah* and Lilith, but more closely between light and dark, passive and active. Contemporary Jewish-American poets often use the Lilith image in just such a fashion. In such a perspective, she beomes indefinable and unfixed. Jerome Rothenberg, in "History One," suggests the possible transformations of Lilith when Lilith reveals all her names to the scholar who wishes to become a saint:

LILITH	ABITR	ABITO	AMORFO
KKODS	IKPODO	AYYLO	PTROTA
ABNUKTA	STRINA	KALI	PTUZA
	TLTOI-PRITSA.[22]		

Rothenberg's manipulations of letters here owes something to the kind of Abulafian letter manipulation of which he is so fond (discussed fully in Chapter 4). Rothenberg insists here that Lilith is not a single being, that she changes forms and essences as she changes names. The female is essentially mutable.

An examination of five different versions of Lilith in five different poets might indicate the various reactions to this image of the first woman. Donald Finkel's "Lilith," a quite predictable and negative portrait, describes her as snakelike and destructive.[23] Her underlying sexual attractiveness and its concommitant temptation form the most striking features of Jascha Kessler's "Waiting for Lilith." Here Lilith's song rises above the ocean of Eve and the sound of family.[24] Howard Schwartz's "Lilith" develops her as defender of unborn children.[25] But some versions of Lilith are almost entirely sympathetic. For instance, Ruth Feldman, in "Lilith," sees her as the complete woman whose beauty men question. She becomes the object of men's lust and the bearer of their illegitimate children, children who do not prosper, but die.[26] Allen Grossman's "Lilith," an even more sympathetic female image, weeps first and she weeps alone. Representing life and sexuality in nature, however, she is extremely powerful:

> I am Lilith, the unmarried,
> Whom three strong angels could not haul
> Back to Eden.
> Let Adam howl like a whipped child,
> The loss was my loss.
> I kneel upon the bank, and take my hair down
> Weeping like a woman,
> Let exiles and altarless men worship me
> As night without stars.
> I spread my hair over them.[27]

By spreading her hair protectively over men, she appropriates that position of solace for the exilic Jews that her supposed opposite, the *Shekinah*, more often assumes.

Lil, the long poem by David Meltzer, is perhaps the most complex use of the Lilith image in contemporary Jewish-American poetry. Praising Meltzer's version of Lilith, Jerome Rothenberg recognizes her as a significant source of poetic inspiration for Meltzer:

as you saw Lilith
equal woman
power in the earth
of good & evil still
persisting
a poetry of changes.[28]

In *Hero/Lil*, Meltzer speaks of Lilith as "process," "song," "First Woman," "Last Woman," "Hag," and "Samael's Whore."[29] She is at the same time one of the brides of God, and the object of human sexual temptation. In places, she becomes a true "she-demon" (p. 42), in places a human whore. But in places she becomes the poet's guide to wisdom:

Lili makes me read Creeley
With greater care,
new clarity (p. 51).

She later even accosts Rashi for Meltzer. In conclusion, Meltzer presents her as part of a mystic unity when he writes

Into the Hay of her, the Hay within the Hay within the Hay of her, as thru door after door of her. All combinations of her interchange. Face into face. Sex into sex. All sparks & specks sing a multitude of possibility. Into the Hay of her, the Hay within the Hay within the Hay of her (p. 80).

The power of speech is given the male, but the power of life is given the woman. For Meltzer writes,

At night I touch her mouth with language. Afterwards I move against her. . . . Law is reversed at night, black is white & white black. She wants words only after sunrise. I touch her mouth with language. Afterwards I move against her (p. 83).

The power of the symbolic contrast of these female images, the inspirational significance of angelic communication, and the weakened effectiveness of prophecy, explains why poets have been drawn to using these types in their poetry. These symbols explain the exile and the pain of present existence. Since the human condition is merely part of a cosmic condition, a single remedy for both will do. There is solace for man in the songs of angels, the words of the prophet, and the love of the *Shekinah*.

Another myth that funds an allegorical construct in contemporary Jewish-American poetry is the Lurianic myth of *tsimtsim*, *shevirah ha-Kelim*, and *tikkun*. In the most extensive example of this use, Howard Schwartz's *Gathering the Sparks*, the complete cosmogonic myth elucidates the poet's commentary on human existence. The dual structure of the book echoes the myth: the first section, "Gathering the Sparks," includes poems that emphasize man's aspiration for redemption; the second section, "Vessels," includes poems of individual human and semidivine moral vessels of God's light. Close analysis of several of these short lyrics will further illustrate Schwartz's interest in Lurianic *kabbalah*.

The title poem, "Gathering the Sparks," begins with an image of precreation, "Long before the sun cast a shadow/Before the Word was spoken."[30] In this prehistory, even then the power to create existed:

> A flame emerged
> From a single
> Unseen
> Point
> And from the center of this flame
> Sparks of light sprang forth
> Concealed in shells (p. 16).

Vessels set sail through the universe, but the vessels break, scattering light everywhere:

> Like sand
> Like seeds
> Like stars (p. 16).

These similes suggest the mystical significance of the sparks: they are numberless; they are sources of life and light; and they are inspiration and guidance. For Schwartz, humanity has one purpose in its creation: to participate in *tikkun* by discovering the lost sparks and becoming reunited with them by being consumed in their fire. The poem ends with the promise of the redemption. When all has been restored,

> And the Word
> Will be spoken
> Again (p. 17).

In "The Temple Vessels," the poet begins with an image of an ancient, holy, and hidden place. Holiness (that is, divine sparks) has been hidden until an earthquake exposes mouldering vessels and fading mirrors. According to the apocalyptic, of course, catastrophe offers hope, for it precedes the messianic advent. The return of the banished sparks would end the exile. In Schwartz's vision,

> The temple will stand restored
> In the center of the city
> And a stream will flow
> From under the Ark
> That will cross the earth
> Uncovering treasures
> That have been hidden
> For centuries
> Until at last
> The waters of this stream
> Flow together
> With those that have their source
> East of Eden (p. 49).

Prelapsarian and postlapsarian waters combine for the messianic time. The restitution of the Temple will realign fallen existence with prelapsarian innocence. Redeemed mankind, "the jewel/In the crown of the King," the image which ends the poem, reflects the light of God.

"The Palace of Shattered Vessels" also depends on the positive outcome of Lurianic cosmic destruction. The fallen sparks are the seeds from which redemption grows. The promise is continual. Refuting one of the central images of twentieth-century western literary tradition, Schwartz describes the landscape,

Not wasteland
But inverted forest
With all the foliage
Underground (p. 50).

The promise of restitution lies in the activity of mankind and, for Howard Schwartz, mankind functions in two ways. Man is clearly the active principle that retrieves, returns, and restores. But he also is one of the vessels that was too frail to hold the light. In other words, he is also a passive principle in the myth of *shevirah ha-Kelim*. In "Vessels," Schwartz describes human beings as clay creations of a physical mother and father, baked in the light of day and lit by the light of night, with the purpose of continuing physical life and the divine spark that is more than physical life. Sexual reproduction assumes cosmic significance, reaffirming that universal force that gave life in the beginning. By losing one's sense of oneself, man is able

To receive
And to transmit,
To grow transparent
In the hour of the offering,
The sacred time
Between two ceremonies
When at last
The pool can be replenished,
When you walk around me
Seven times
And I begin to glow (p. 97).

Another contemporary Jewish-American poet, David Meltzer, also refers to the Lurianic myth of *tsimtsim*, *shevirah ha-Kelim*, and *tikkun*. In a collection of poetry, *A Midrash*, section one comments on Psalm 119:

Remember the word unto Thy servant
Because Thou has made me to hope.
This is my comfort in my affliction,
That Thy word hath quickened me.[31]

Sparks appear throughout this poem. Meltzer begins his commentary with an awareness that whenever he shuts his eyes, he sees sparks. When he was born, he was aware of leaving sparks behind with his mother. His poetic commentary centers on the figures of two men: his Uncle Lable Leshinsky, a glazier, newly become wallet maker, who, in a previous incarnation, was a Lurianic pupil and a rabbi who teaches David. Often the two older men become one for

> The Rabbi is tall, fat, small, lean, rat-like, a
> fox, an owl,
> a cloud in space with bloody lips, he inhales night (p. 142).

The rabbi's face and his body are made of sparks and he tells his pupil to "Study each spark. . . . In each spark is a letter of the book you yearn to read" (p. 142). The poet, Meltzer, then must turn to these divine sparks that make up nature in order to discover his own poetics. He identifies himself as the translator of the rabbi's Lurianic *kabbalah*. In the words of the poet, he says

> A single spark is a letter wed to another letter until a word is
> formed. A single world is a word I spend days travelling thru (p.
> 143).

Just as the rabbi sees men as "seed-sparks of Him" (p. 144), as creatures in God's image, so does Uncle Lable try to formulate images of import in his craft, "pouring moulds with strange stuff he later turns into letters that are prisms that are magic weapons against darkness, the enemy" (p. 143). Now an automaton in an American assembly line, his uncle

> . . . once . . . was a glazier in Safed
> . . . .
> Once he made letters of glass that were prisms
> that were secret lenses
> to read between lines of a bird song
> to capture exaltation's first birth lights (p. 145).

Uncle Lable is as much a Lurianic *kabbalist* as the rabbi. When the rabbi turns to the poet singing the Yiddish song "Raisins and Almonds," the poet's heart breaks, for Meltzer knows he cannot accomplish his teachers' wishes; he cannot gather all the sparks, for redemption has not arrived. The poet breaks into splinters and cries about the Jew's contemporary and newer exile near the Moldau:

> Foam of impact fragments into angels & demons rising like Dachau smoke into the sky, into Paradise. Fuel for voices. Context & balance for the souls we share between us (p. 146).

All the Jews of history unite in a final image of death and destruction as well as peoplehood. The Lurianic cosmogonic myth hereby describes an allegorical pattern for the tale of mankind's movement through history to salvation.

Contemporary Jewish-American poetry uses another symbolic pattern that derives from the apocalyptic: historical epochs to imply ages of man and qualities of time. Usually cyclical and always typological, apocalyptic historical patterns sometimes appear in Jewish-American poetry in autobiographical terms. The idea of exile and return, the pattern that apocalypse describes, structures these poems. One example of the symbolic exile develops from the typology of a biblical character and his multiple appearances in history. In "Exile," Anthony Hecht compares the exiles of three historical Josephs: Joseph of Genesis, Joseph, husband of Mary in the Christian New Testament, and Joseph Brodsky, the Soviet Jewish poet who was exiled from Russia in 1972 for writing decadent and socially unacceptable poetry. Hecht writes the poem for Brodsky, to remind him that as a Jew he has been here before. First he was sold into bondage in Egypt. Through his prophetic ability to interpret dreams, he saved himself. Second, he traveled with his wife and child, "the child not yours,/The wife, whom you adored, in a way not yours."[32] This Joseph's life was harder than the first Joseph's life and he cannot remember much of it, perhaps only the birth and that "Mixed with an obscure and confusing music,/Confused with a smell of hay and steaming dung." The family was lost, lost of course to the historical Joseph, but also to the Jewish tradition as the Christian followers transformed the story beyond all Jewish recognition, transforming it more into a story in a Greek mystery cult. The third Joseph, who moved to Michigan as poet in residence at the university, must come to terms with another kind of exile, but an exile nevertheless. Surrounded by the expressionless faces of people in Walker Evans photographs, his living conditions are those of urban life—weeds, dishwater poured out of kitchen windows, wheezing chimneys, and hydrangeas. As Hecht admonishes Brodsky,

> This is Egypt, Joseph, the old school of the soul.
> You will recognize the rank smell of a stable
> And the soft patience in a donkey's eyes,
> Telling you you are welcome and at home.

Politics damns the promise of return, the messianic advent must wait. All the Josephs can return from their Egypts to their real homes only after the Messiah appears. D. H. Lawrence's delayed gratification plays a significant role in this poem.

More often than not, however, the American-Jewish poet writes of his own history as a symbol of the classic Jewish patterns of exile and return. For instance, Irving Feldman, in *Works and Days*, likens his autobiography to the historical chronology of the Jewish people. Personally exiled from his past, Feldman only returns to his family and Judaism through personal trauma. Exile and return form the structure of the entire long poem, and the sections that most clearly reveal the apocalyptic version of this pattern are, quite appropriately, the first, "The Ark," and two later ones, "Apocalypse" and "Crystal" (the last of which is the last section of the poem and part of a subsection of a larger division entitled "Return").[33] "The Ark" describes the poet's upbringing in a ghetto, depression-marked family where he "learned all history's a *pogrom*" (p. 35). Unlike for the Christian, violence was not a Jew's method of defense. Only the Wailing Wall and the promise of the Temple's rebuilding could defend a Jew. The passivity, poverty, and frugality of his life in the ghetto combine with the Jew's sense of special election:

> Free of the flood, our ghetto tied
> Smugly to the rope of His wrath,

> We thought to put the world aside
> Like the dirty ring after a bath (p. 35).

Specific images of his home, his mother, and his father, reenforce the oppressive existence and sacrifice he felt in his childhood. Death seemed the only absolute promise in life. Finally, the poet chose self-imposed exile; he fled from

> The old rock, the old ark
> Hung aloft on Ararat—
> Crow lost in a world of wrack (p. 37).

At his departure from the Jewish past, he leaves as a crow not a dove. He will not bring back glad tidings, but tales of death. He flies away from the ark: Noah's ark, the ark of the Covenant, and the ark which houses the Torah, that ties the Jew to the promise of the people's redemption. The ark in Feldman's life awaits his eventual return to tradition—much as the covenant of God, the Messiah, awaits the ingathering of exiles for the messianic advent.

In "Apocalypse," the bright, loud, and crowded images of New York City impinge on the poet. The world outside, that world of "Wrack," begins to disintegrate. Storms attack the ship, not an ark in this section, and a "prodigal crow" must decide whether or not to fly out to see if all is secure. Feldman has maintained his tie to the Jewish past only through the "wraith/Of chickens all those Fridays" (p. 46), an ironic reference to the gastronomic Jew who remembers the traditional Friday night meal of roasted chicken but forgets to light the candles. But the ghosts of death begin to trouble the poet, and he feels no longer capable of perceiving subjects worthy of poetry:

> And then I saw the ark adrift
> Under a sodden sky. I grinned
> And thought, Return. Like a handkerchief
> Its sail stood diapering the wind (p. 47).

Feldman chooses to return to his past and sees the ark cradling the nature around him.

Out of practice with touching his past, he mistakes his feelings of love for his parents for sentimentality and "useless pity." Yet in the very last section, "Crystal," Feldman comes to terms with his past and his need to return. Like Lot's wife, he turns to salt when he looks back at his past, but the ark, his past, does not remain the same. It bursts like an apple spilling seeds; his past, not of value in itself, becomes valuable in its ability to fertilize this imagination. Through the past as a crystal, and himself transformed to a crystal through his tears (that is, salt), Feldman can write worthy poetry, but only as a novice for

> Scratch . . . scratch. I came tapping the stone,
> Blind remembering, blind with tears, scratching my grief
> In the stone, blind wounds on the tomb of light.
> Tap tap. And who will let me in? Shall
> The crystal open, the ground awake, the dreamers rise? (p. 51)

He raises a bifurcated question: whether or not the dead will be resurrected, and whether or not he will gain the insight afforded only the initiates of the apocalyptic school.

Two poems by American Jews use the Christian legend of Wandering Jew to describe their individual exile/return histories as types for the Jew. Appropriately enough, these two poems also concern themselves with the problem of assimilation. Both Irving Feldman and Robert Mezey entitle their poems "Wandering Jew," and, in fact, the title of Mezey's collection which includes the individual poem is the same. Feldman articulates the Jewish resistance to assimilation to the Christian culture as a necessary resistance in order to attain appropriate prophetic powers. Mezey, on the other hand, seems much less optimistic about the possibility of such resistance. In fact, Mezey finds the identification with Jewishness necessary in order to resist assimilation as not particularly attractive; he calls the contemporary Jewish-American's sense of his Jewish past a "squalid ghost."[34]

Feldman's "Wandering Jew" is a poem in five parts: "The Gates of Gaza," "The Face of God," "The Wailing Wall," "Assimilation," and "Scratch,"[35] The first section, beginning with a reference to the pain of being a Jew in exile ("*O Jerusalem, if I forget thee, may I die!//If I forget thee not, how will I live!*" [p. 94]), centers on Samson's city of Gaza, here representing exilic burden. The despair of building Jerusalem in a fallen world appears in the ending stanza. In the "Face of God," Feldman writes of the divinity of everyday love and events—the cooking of meals, the Sabbath, and the *yahrzeit* candle. But also the melancholy of the Jewish existence permeates the scenes:

> And now I wander accused by that Sinai
> In a glass, by muteness of our closest wish,
> By a God humble, tiny, and good. And I
> Choke with pathos of a clean dish (p. 95).

As suggested in the poem cited earlier, *Works and Days*, for Irving Feldman the Wailing Wall represents Jewish solace. In keeping with this image, in the section "The Wailing Wall," Feldman calls on God to protect him from the pains of exile. The particulars of Irving Feldman's life (born the year before the stock market crash, a father who went bankrupt, life in Brooklyn in the lower-middle class, and his freckled and bespectacled person) provide the basis for the poet's complaint against God. How can a Jew be a hero if he is expected only to suffer and complain? Where is God as protector of the Jews when Irving Feldman loses job opportunities, lawsuits, and conflicts with landlords? Only at the Wailing Wall, however, could the poet as Jew expect God to hear these individual pains. In full consciousness of the irony of the request, Feldman ends this section: "Bend closer, my God, I can complain till all the stars drown" (p. 97).

From complaints of God's oversight, Feldman turns to the even more painful recognition of the temptation of assimilation and assimilation's reduction of God's communication with his Chosen People. "Assimilation" dreams of Heaven, but the dream is filled with the images of the assimilated Jew: pinochle, checkers, the Ed Sullivan Show, Ed Murrow, Miami Beach, Grauman's Chinese theatre, Macy's, Grossinger's, Atlantic City, dirty old men, Loew's theatre, and the Lone Ranger. The section ends with the oppressiveness of assimilation:

And it's always dark and everything's free and you never hear No.
But I can't breathe and think I'll drown in the stuff and
                    nobody'll know.
And I wake up kicking and screaming, Lemme go!
                    Lemme go! (p. 99)

In the final section of the poem, as in *Works and Days*, God's communication sounds like a scratch and the prophet, the Jew, returning
to his Jewish identity is a blind man tapping the stone. The poet
asks God all the hard questions: how can he live, how can he be
prepared for the Messiah, how can he speak God's word, how can he
resist the devil, and how can he find God Himself? God's only
answer is a series of vowel changes of "Scratch": "Scretch," "Scritch,"
"Scrotch," "Scrutch," "Screetch," "Scrautch," "Scroatch," and
"Scratch" (pp. 100–101). God's communication with man seems
mysterious under the best of circumstances. But if the man has
abandoned his election, has denied his Jewish identity, has
assimilated, then the communication becomes unintelligible. And
the inevitable result is the delay of the messianic advent.

    In the collection *Wandering Jew* Robert Mezey echoes much of
the pain and the desire for belief about which Irving Feldman writes.
However, Mezey is more skeptical of success. In "Against Seasons,"
he questions why we should praise the natural order of things or the
desire for the messianic solution or in fact any solution for the present situation. He does not respect the apocalyptic answer:

    They say a shattering horn will blow,
    They say we must not be afraid,
    But they are fools for saying so.
    Endless meridians swing and fade (p. 59).

In fact, Mezey sees no end to chronological time. Yet, the poet
waits, "Tired of God and of God's work." Prophecy in such a disillu-
sioned state is painful, but irresistible. In "With My God the Smith"
Mezey writes

    Like chapters of prophecy my days burn, in all the revelations,
    And my body between them's a block of metal for smelting,
    And over me stands my God the Smith, who hits hard (p. 62).

God as the smith works on the prophetic spirit of the ˉpoet. His beating is hard but true and results in the wounds of time. When the poet's mouth becomes "an open wound," then God offers him a night of rest.

Mezey's poem "Wandering Jew," like Feldman's poem, clearly bases the evaluation of the Jewish-American condition on the facts and details of an individual Jewish-American life. Mezey's life follows a pattern similar to that of Feldman in *Works and Days*: birth into a life of traditional Jewish ritual, Sabbath wine, prayer shawls, the ark, the sense of poverty in the ghetto; passage through a period of denial of the Jewish past; a time in Egypt with its sense of God's unforgiveable silence; and finally a sort of return to Jewish identity. Mezey feels his bondage to assimilation, chaffs under the bitterness of exile, sickens at the images of the Holocaust as the most recent and most powerful example of Gentile anti-Semitism, and questions God's plan for the Jew:

> Reeking with gas, they hint what ancient fame,
> What mad privation made them what they are,
> . . . .
> A flock of people prey to every horror,
> Scattered by thirty centuries of war,
> The sport of Christian duke and Hauptsturmfuehrer—
> Is this the covenant we were chosen for? (p. 70)

Nature itself becomes a memorial to the Jewish dead and God mourns his people. As a Jew, Mezey writes of inheriting a "barren mountain and [an] empty sky." He tries to find the answer in Torah, senses his unworthiness, and in disillusionment turns from *Halakah*, but not without a lesson learned. Though he will study Torah no more, he discovers a metaphysic, "*Live*, says the Law," and Mezey writes "I sit here doing my best,/Relishing meat, listening to music" (p. 71). It is a minimal metaphysic, but its attention to life and to the present is Judaic. The Feldman hope of a divine communication, even though it be a "Scratch," is missing in Mezey.

The search for the messianic advent is fraught with danger and pain. In fact, in the most traditional apocalyptic descriptions preceding the Messiah's appearance, the pains of the Messiah's birth indicates horrifying times of wars and destruction. As painful as the suffering of the exiled Jews be at the present, the suffering must increase in order to usher in the end of time. However, the response to the Holocaust by the contemporary western Jew, particularly the American Jew, marks a transformation of that traditional expectation of the disintegration of the present situation of the Jews. The example of such grotesque and calculated methods of anti-Semitism perpetrated by such a civilized culture evoked two contradictory responses. As can be seen particularly in the poetry of Robert Mezey, God is condemned for his retreat from history, for his silence. The messianic hope is an illusion, for nothing could justify the ovens of Auschwitz; nothing could redeem mankind after the ovens. The other response is that surely the messianic advent is near, for never before have the Jews suffered so deeply. Zionists cite the reestablishment of the political state of Israel, a rather literal representation of the return of the exiles, as further proof of the immanence of the Messiah. The symbolic translation of actor and event, however, indicates a conscious attempt by the author to overcome the specificity of history. The allegorical interpretations of the apocalyptic do not provide a moral comment on a contemporary event or explain the pain of the present by the hope of the future. The allegorical mode removes the specificity of history, allowing man to see himself and his leaders as types in a long caravan toward the goal of the messianic advent.

Chapter 4

The Messianic Ontology

The most abstract symbolic constructs found in contemporary Jewish-American literature influenced by apocalyptic messianism follow two *kabbalistic* patterns. First, the *kabbalistic*, especially Lurianic, emanation theory strove to explain how and why things were the way they were in the exile. The Lurianic cosmogonic myth, as discussed in the previous chapter, forms the outline for this theory, but the theory can be understood to explain more than creation itself, indeed to explain the nature of man and the nature of his relationship to God (through His *sephira*). Second, *kabbalistic*, especially Abulafian, *gematria* emphasizes the cosmic value of each Hebrew letter in apprehending the universe.[1] Both of these theories appear as prominent influences in contemporary Jewish-American poetry—in Susan Mernit, John Hollander, Jerome Rothenberg, and David Meltzer. Susan Mernit divides the world into spiritualized divisions that share terms and ideas with traditional *kabbalistic* versions of the *sephira*; John Hollander divides the white light of existence into the seven component aspects of white that parallel the seven branches of the menorah in the second Temple and the seven heavenly bodies of Philo's versions of the universe. Jerome Rothenberg describes modern mystical patterns as messianic reincarnation. David Meltzer equates spiritual and aesthetic mentorship. All of these poets and several others try to present answers to the basic ontological questions of existence in the *kabbalistic* language of Isaac Luria or Abraham Abulafia.

In Susan Mernit's *The Angelic Alphabet*, the first four sections tell of the hidden emanations of the Lurianic universe, the next five represent the revealed emanations, and the final three offer some conclusive statement on emanations in man's existence. The first four are entitled with Hebrew words for spiritual aspects of the *Ein Sof*. The imagistic "Nephesch" (soul) suggests intangible aspects of nature—fog and aroma. It ends

> Nephesch
>
>> the body rises
>
> plastic and supple
> from the core
>
> Over all language
>
>> of water
>
> the land eases itself with joy.[2]

The images of "Guph" (body) display a more material presence. In this section, spices evoking aroma and water causing fog remind the reader of the more insubstantial nature of the previous section. In "Ruach" (ghost), filled with violent images of life, blood is particularly apparent. It ends "Today/the blood comes" to indicate menses. Rather than the blood of death, then, Mernit writes of the blood of life. Cosmic images that transform individual human death into life permeate the final hidden part of the universe "Neschamah" (soul).

Mernit's decision to open the revealed section with the tenth emanation, "Malkuth," God's most physical emanation into nature, rather than the sixth intensifies the shocking juxtaposition of these most abstract of images with the revealed emanations of Lurianic cosmogony. Beginning with the Garden of Eden and ending with the four directions of the world (East, West, South, North) described in relation to the elements of creation ("wind of trees," "water on land," "blood on the river," and "quickening light"), this section is quite concrete. For emanation nine, "Yesod" (foundation), also concrete, human significance prevails. Mernit repeats the garden image, but with the addition of particular flowers and other facts of nature—violet, crocus, narcissus, lovers, and leaves. The lovers, their sexual desire, and consequent coupling, in fact, become central, suggesting the vital relationship of man to the emanation of God. The fertile female presence hints at the Lurianic *kabbalah*. For Mernit, only woman offers humankind the ability to live fully in the garden:

> and you are living
> on an island
> you have emptied
> this land
>
> this garden.

"Hod" (majesty) reenforces the sexual nature of the female principle, but by being unable to speak, she seems more restricted. The sexual encounter shines and the male figure reminds the reader of *Adam Kadmon*, "The Heavenly Man." In the seventh emanation, "Netsach" (victory), the woman's sexual power appears in images alluded to in earlier sections. In other words, the female becomes the revealed emanation of *Ein Sof*. She becomes a creature that can reform man. The sun that burned in the previous section now brings the moon into view; the male principle has given way to the female. Finally, "Tipheras" refers to the cyclical nature of life, particularly as evidenced in the physical being of womankind. The sun image in the section fades into the moon image, the feminine principle "flooding the world." Woman overwhelms existence.

The final three sections echo images developed in the hidden and revealed emanations of the earlier nine—the garden, the sun, the moon, mirrors, water, and blood. In the later sections, the poet focuses on her own individual consciousness. Susan Mernit presents her own technique of working the emanation theory into her poetics. She begins in "Techniques for Craftsmen" by saying that poets must look for this garden

> where the world
> is no symbol
>   but union
> of branch and root.

This is a world, then, where the hidden and revealed unite. Whereas the woman in "Netsach" had been "crystal/inside the mirror," and the elements of East, West, South, and North were divided, now all creation becomes

> a single sheet
> area of space
> cold to the hand:
>
> the lake of silver
> as mirror
>
> the liquid mirror
> as water
>
> and the water as base,
> root of the tree
>
> opaque crystal
> at base root.

Thus, after full division and description of each emanation, Mernit turns back to the *Ein Sof*, the union of all creation in the root. "Notes about the Root" and "Working the Root" tell of the mystery of all existence in the source of all life—"deep inside the heart." A tree grows from a root, so does all of life grow from *Ein Sof*. The Old English "wort," meaning root, is important in its magical herbal abilities to ward off evil, as well as its denotation as foundation. *Ein Sof*, another wort, gives us support and protection. By using an English word, Mernit conveys the idea that the foundational principle of all of nature does not remain merely a Hebrew enterprise. In the final section, Mernit describes man's sexual nature, the universe's cyclical pattern, and the physical existence of the plant world as mere patterns of *Ein Sof* for

> the axis
> of the world descends
> · · · · · · ·
> yielding not root
> but branch.

Man sees not the root, but the emanation. Man sees, in fact, godhead, for all these physical presences express the root in the firmness and substantiality of stone.

John Hollander, another example of the influence of emanation theory on contemporary Jewish-American poetry, is not usually thought of in the context of any ethnic group. Though much of his literature surely bespeaks a generalized western culture, individual poems in his canon derive much of their power from his knowledge of Jewish esoteric sources. One of the most interesting of these is the long poem *Spectral Emanations*. The very title, "emanations," suggests a reference to Lurianic *kabbalah* and its cosmology based on varying emanations of *Ein Sof*. Hollander affirms the clearly Jewish-American content of this poem "in seven branches in lieu of a lamp," by the headnote which reminds the reader of Josephus's description of the golden lamp of the Second Temple, and then quotes from Nathaniel Hawthorne's *Marble Faun* where Miriam says of the Temple candelabra:

> *There was a meaning and purpose in each of its seven branches, and such a candlestick cannot be lost forever. When it is found again, and seven lights are kindled and burning in it, the whole world will gain the illumination which it needs. Would not this be an admirable idea for a mystic story or parable, or seven-branched allegory, full of poetry, art, philosophy, and religion? . . . As each branch is lighted, it shall have a differently colored lustre from the other six; and when all seven are kindled, their radiance shall combine into the white light of truth.* [3]

For Hollander, the seven candles described in Josephus and Hawthorne are of different colors, different sounds, and express different attitudes. Hollander's headnote indicates what the form of the poem will be: a prologue and then the colored sections, "*starting with the red cry of battle, followed by the false orange gold, true yellow goldenness, the green of all our joy, blue of our imaginings, the indigo between and the final violet that is next to black, for that is how our scale runs. Below each cup of color is a branch of prose, following and supporting it*" (p. 3). Therefore, prose commentary follows each colored poetic section. Of the other structural features explicated by Hollander in

his notes, the most significant to the *kabbalistic* influence involves
his use of seven sections each with seventy-two lines of poetry. The
numerological symbolism of seven arises from the seven-branched
candelabra and Hollander suggests in his notes that the seventy-two
lines per section are a function of an equal division of factorial seven
(that is, 504) (p. 229). Other particularly Jewish interpretations of
seventy-two add to Hollander's number game. First, according to
Talmud, the menorah to which Hollander refers was in fact seventy-
two inches high.[4] The number has rabbinic and ritualistic
significance. Furthermore we should not overlook the tradition of
the seventy-two letter name of God (discussed in Chapter 1).
Therefore, form and content of *Spectral Emanations* issue from *kabbalah*. The review of this poem by Harold Bloom seems most accurate in distinguishing the style toward which Hollander strives:
"Hollander has developed into an American-Jewish High Romantic,
esoteric and elegiac, and daring to write long poems in the Sublime
mode."[5] The very style of *Spectral Emanations* is *kabbalistic*.

The Prologue, "The Way to the Throne Room," leads
Hollander's initiate from Babylon ("the captive shore") to an inner
sanctum (pp. 5–7). Questioned at each step, the initiate refers to differing angels of differing traditions (that is, Hebrew, Indo-European,
and idiosyncratic) who perform duties in guiding his initiation.
However, on the way to the seventh chamber, something happens,
and he is not allowed to enter the chamber. Initiation has failed.

The "Red" emanation of war and Mars draws many images from
the 1973 Yom Kippur War, the time during which Hollander wrote
this section. "J," the creature who fights and dies during the conflict,
parallels Jonah as "J is exceedingly/Glad of the gourd"—though J's
gourd does not protect (p. 7). The images of peace in this first section seem to be only derivations of violence: the "Tender olive bird"
is "plucked/Out of Leviathan"; J hears "The fierce ghost of his sire"
in his fight in the desert and he is awakened from his slumber with
the rocket that is

        . . . the fiery worm:
        Unwilling prophet of
        His past (p. 8).

In the final lines of the poetic part of "Red," J is eviscerated and he literally becomes part of the earth, an identity that is reenforced by the similarity of the Hebrew words for man (*Adam*) and blood (*Adom*):

> Blood, rooted in earth,makes
> Adam's kingdom, Adam,
> Fruit brought forth of iron,
> The wide realm of the red (p. 9).

The prose section of "Red" further develops the play on Hebrew words by the allusion to the pictogram source of the consonants that make up the Hebrew words previously cited: "Aleph" is derived from a pictogram for "ox," "Daleth" from a pictogram for "door," and "Mem" from a pictogram for "water." In these mundane sources for the color of war, Hollander writes of the power of warfare to transform all that man sees and experiences. The Isaiah promise of ploughshares seems very far away in "Red," rather the obverse seems accurate. However, in this emanation, the perceptive initiate can look to another place and time:

> The red singer sits looking back toward the violet becoming black. His songs are capable of the opened and the spilled; only for them the wind sings in his hair. He stands outside the door: his shadow falls across it. Blown dust makes a false threshold (p. 10).

Midas and Jupiter govern the second emanation, "Orange." This "age of awakening" denies the promise of gold:

> Drops of orange juice that Midas
> Thirsts for are turned into burning
> Bullets (p. 11).

Usually man chooses lead over gold, transforming gold as Circe transformed men. Inversions of value are typical of this emanation. Gold is, according to the angel of this emanation (Roy G. Biv), "a dream of lead," and "All the colors are fractions of white" (p. 12).

The section ends with a parody of a Hebrew prayer that blesses the one who brings forth *"fruit of the bronze: bells and pomegranates, thunder and lightning"* (p. 13).

In Saturn's emanation, "Yellow," golden images of nature, forsythia and jonquils, for instance, prophesy more to come. But

> It would remain an interpretation
> Of the flimsy text, half unremembered,
> Dimming evermore and diminishing (p. 13).

Hollander equates the promise of each season and of the special quality of Sabbath with yellow, echoing the Hebrew prayers that thank God for bringing the individual to this season and to the special peace of the day of rest.[6] Gold contains colors to come (such as blue) and colors already seen (such as red), but the distinctness of gold remains: "The dark lines of goldenness afire" (p. 15). In his description of the heroic glory of a Thomas Cole painting, *The Course of Empire*, in which Mars is mistaken for Saturn ("gatherer of red rather than of yellow" [p. 16]), Hollander presents a tradition of confused values. In keeping with this failure of vision and perception, the poet ends this section of hopeful redemptive yellow with a reminder of the power of Miriam's paintings in Hawthorne's *Marble Faun*. Her copies were better than the originals: "It was not that it was a copy, nor that it was not even after some lost original. It was that it was hers. This was true plenty" (p. 16). This, a replica in sound of the lost menorah of the Second Temple, strives toward the excellence of Miriam's reproductions. Not only can the viewer not depend on the value of what seems gold not to be a "travesty of value," as it appeared in the "Orange" section, but also he must realize that perhaps the re-creation might attain more value than the original.

"Green" is the central pole of the menorah and the realm of the sun. Because of its greater stability, Hollander tells us in the headnote that *"Only at the moment of green is there time for a story, for only that branch is vertical, the other supports being parabolic"* (p. 3). This story, the most imaginative and fertile portion of "Green," follows poetry which describes simple natural beauty and vitality. "Green" describes an emanation of stasis and comfort. The story, however, implies movement; it relates the search of seven people: Werth, Gelb, Krasny, Sagol, Pomaranczowy, Kuan, and the unnamed narrator.[7] These conspirators try to discover the replicas of the menorah and destroy them, but their decision to destroy is not a contented one. For instance, the narrator sees the contemporary green of the summer in which they search as fading into "the days of autumn waiting before me, of the impending grays and browns. . . . And my vision must narrow to the task" (p. 29). In other words, he must reject the statsis and sensuality of green in order to act, in order to destroy. Further, his vision is not a complete one; it is a lamed vision (p. 29):

> It is not even the view toward the Pisgah from which the hedged promise of the to-be-arrived-at will gleam, to, but not for, the climber in the sunset. It is not the binocular seizure of detail, nor the important zoom into what matters for the task at hand. It is not of reaching height; it is not of squat failure. It is of the surroundingness (p. 30).

Though the vision from "Green" interprets and reassesses, the travelers should not trust the vision completely, for it does not even offer the sight of Moses into the Promised Land.

In "Blue," the emanation of the planet and god Mercury, moons, and "drafty lamplight" dominate. Night is not completely dark, for the blue is the blue that precedes such darkness. The different possible blues and the different meanings of these blues suggest the indefinable nature of this emanation. The sky and the ocean are literally tied, for instance, in an image where "a blue moon setting dipped/Deep in the broad water, dyeing it" (p. 31). Blue and yellow, the two emanations that surround the green of the sun, are equals and opposites. Therefore, the coldness of blue and its mystic light counterbalance the bright promise of gold. Man's nighttime false methods of light attempt to nullify this blue, for the true vision of this emanation can come only at dawn when

> . . . we distinguish blue from—white?
> No, green—and, in agreement, eyeing the
> Dying dark, our morning wariness nod (p. 33).

In the daylight, man fears his surroundings more than at night. The prose section of "Blue" emphasizes the danger of the man-made light, for man must not deny this blue either in its darkness, its color, or its materiality. As Hollander writes:

> The mercury is another matter: its drops cohere so—oily but dry, like seeds of gleaming—cold sparks hinting of the tiny hot planet. It will get out of hand; yet it is absolutely essential to the working (p. 33).

In fact, then, the mercury suggests to the poet the very sparks of creation that Lurianic *kabbalah* presents as essential means of redemption. To avoid or deny this emanation is to deny redemption.

"Departed Indigo," the emanation of Venus, expresses feminine beauty and attractiveness. Whether she appears as the "gracious, kind and hooded/Lady" of the poet's father (p. 34), the "fragile virgin of Justice" (p. 34), Madame de Violet, or Frau Blau (p. 35), she represents Venus. In color, she stands somewhere between the "blue of day/Sky, and the violet of night" (p. 35). Promising both blue and violet emanations and the combination of these emanations, she stands,

> Now, in the regions of vision
> Where she dwells—not like that first frail
> Maiden who fled into starlight,
> A mere novel constellation,
> But between these touching points of
> Light—the rich, hopeful darkness seems
> Deepened by her presence, under
> Which we live and, hushed, still breathe the
> Night air's perfume of discernment (p. 36).

Similar to the feminine principle so important in Lurianic *kabbalah*, Hollander's Venus controls and redefines the vision of *Spectral Emanations*. In the prose section of "Departed Indigo," he recapitulates the previous six sections of the poem and the types of heroes associated with each previous age and emanation described:

"At first our heroes stood for us, then among us, when we stood for ourselves; now they do not even represent our sorrows" (p. 37). Even the Bible seems to be destroyed in this our age of indigo.

However, the time of "Violet," emanation of the moon (feminine source of light), offers the consolation of completion and promise in a modern Lurianic redemption. The circularity of time, the sense that man knows at the beginning what will be his end, is clearly the foundational principle of "Violet." But Hollander evokes here not Eliot's sense of timelessness in *The Four Quartets*, but the timelessness of the Jewish apocalyptic. The last violet candle will wane and yet it promises, as reflection of all that preceded, to last beyond the others. However, it can not guide:

> Like a star reflected
> In a cup of water,
> It will light up no path:
>
> Neither will it go out.
> Here at the easternmost
> Edge of the sunset world (p. 39).

Clearly the indicator of death, this light suggests more than individual afterlife, for it becomes

> —A tree of light. A bush
> Unconsumed by its fire.
> Branches of flame given
>
> Sevenfold tongue that there
> Might be recompounded
> Out of the smashed vessels (p. 39).

The burning bush of Genesis represents an inspiration that burns but does not consume itself, similar to the Lurianic myth of creation and salvation out of destruction: *tsimtsim, shevirah ha-kelim*, and *tikkun*. Nature itself, in Hollander, becomes lit and fed by the fallen light. He ends the poem in memories of childhood, memories of color and colorlessness. Chemists' flasks and the colored water in their flasks unleash the following memory:

he was told "Those are colored water" not as if a radiance had been selectively stained, but as if the colorless had been awakened from its long exile in mere transparency.

The diaspora of water ends when those colored bowls give back nothing that is untinted by their own light (p. 41).

Light and color, like the Jews, suffer exile, separation, in a fallen state that is contemporary life. Violet becomes a positive end, and accepting of the limitations of mortality. In fact, Hollander in true Lurianic spirit finally suggests the salvational principle that can only come from destruction: "when we have been stamped out and burned not to lie in the ashes of our dust, it will be to grow" (p. 42).

Even more widely influential in contemporary Jewish-American poetry than emanation theory is letter and number symbolism. Some of the poets indicate a deep appreciation of the specific meditative *kabbalah* of Abulafia, some a more general interest in Hebrew *gematria*, and some use the idea of mystical value of letters in a general understanding of language, the languages being both Hebrew and English.

The influences of letter manipulation and permutation on the poetry of Jack Hirschman are less evident in specific reference to a particular Abulafian system and more evident in reference to the general Jewish tradition of *gematria, notarikon,* and *zeruf.* Manipulation of the values of the alphabet letters as powerful symbols and cosmic forces functions in many of Hirschman's poems and in poems by a goodly number of other contemporary Jewish-American poets. For instance, some of these poets follow the example of celebrating individual qualities in Hebrew letters. Laurence Kusher's *The Book of Letters,* Stuart Z. Perkoff's *alphabet,* and Rose Drachler's "The Letters of the Book" are complete *aleph-bets,* providing various interpretations of the twenty-two letters.[8] Jerome Rothenberg ("*Aleph* Poem," " A Poem for *Ayin*")[9] and Harvey Shapiro ("*Aleph*")[10] write about individual letters; Harvey Shapiro ("Six Hundred Thousand Letters")[11] describes the power of the letters of the alphabet in general, and Emily Borenstein ("Life of the Letters")[12] the music of the letters. A few modern poets experiment widely with the ancient Hebrew alphabetic argumentation and gnostic traditions of *gematria, notarikon,* and *zeruf.*

In the 1971 collection *Knots*, David Meltzer published a ten-section poem entitled "Letters & Numbers" which specifically refers to the mystical numerological system of the *Sepher Yetzirah*, Meltzer's age in life evokes the mystical speculation, for he begins

> In my 32nd year
> counting numbers watching
> 22 letters dance on a wall chart.
> Energy goes in & out of 10
> ineffable sefira.[13]

Mystically equating his own development with the thirty-two paths of the ancient creative numerology, Meltzer describes his life, his sexual encounters with his wife, his apperception of the world around him in a scheme derived from the *Sepher Yetzirah*. He identifies the earth with his wife and further with their couch of consummation. The answer to existence and creativity for man lies in the understanding of the mystic patterns,

> Tracking down 32 lights
> O eternal pinball metaphor
> Electric-eyed whore
> how we serve you
> your round lights
> service all your
> magic numbers! (p. 111).

Meltzer ends the poem by asserting that the mystery lies in silence and in experience. In other words, he sees the mystic response as possible for all who wish to meditate on and thus experience the silences of creation.

Some poets write alphabetical exercises similar to Abraham Abulafia's meditative prophetic technique, but without any specific reference to Abulafia or his writings. These poets include Jerome Rothenberg and Jack Hirschman whose thorough knowledge of the primary texts of Abulafian writing make the argument for the influence of Abraham Abulafia on their speculations on the value of letters and numbers convincing.

Jack Hirschman entitled his collection of poems written from

1960 to 1968, *Black Alephs*, suggesting the Hebraic attention to letters. In this collection several poems refer to the letters of the
Hebrew alphabet and to the morphemes of Hebrew words as a
means of argumentation. In many examples in the collection,
Hirschman cites the letters of the alphabet and their individual
mystical significance. Two of these poems best reveal his attention
to *gematria*, *notarikon*, and *zeruf*. "Fingerpoint" describes the movement of the meditative disciple as he studies the Hebrew text, the
Hebrew letters.[14] The wisdom of the individual will "shine," that is,
will grow, as he watches, hears, and repeats the movements of the
Hebrew consonants, the points that mark vowel pronunciation, and
the accents of the words in the sentence. In Hirschman's images,
the letters are the body, the points the spirit; the letters are the
army, the accents the king. Only the wise one, the mentor, can
guide this movement, even directing the pauses that allow true
understanding of the words. "Ascent," an explicit example of
Hebraic argumentation by careful consideration of the letters of a
text and the etymology of words,[15] revolves around an etymological
argument based on the triad of the Hebrew letters: *Samek* (s), *Feh*
(ph), *Resh* (r). Semitic words are derived from triple consonant
bases; the vowels are insignificant in the analysis of the word's meanings. In "Ascent," the poet argues the derivation of *sapheir*: possible
meanings include number, sphere, permitted to narrate, the end of a
thing. Finally, Hirschmen cites the most famous text of letter symbolism in the Jewish tradition, *Sepher Yetzirah* to which the poet says
Abraham "points/when he says, 'Sephir, Sephar and Siphur.'"
Presumably Hirschman is referring to Abraham Abulafia and his
commentary on the text *Sepher Yetzirah*, directing us to other possible meanings of the triple letters: emanations, books (or the written word), and a city in the Bible. But the poem itself ends with a
final play on the three sounds, in English, from a rabbi in America:

> Rabbi
> Gershom Luria of Brooklyn, on the
> other hand, leaned over and with
> a smile said into my ear:
>   'The brightness ("The
> heavens declare the glory (the brightness) of Elohim")

> is iridescent, in which all colors are
> as a jewel hanging from the neck of Adonai
> in which one sees ten and ten times ten
> billions of sparks in
> sapphire' (p. 36).

The heavens and their color, whether that color be said in Hebrew or in English, express the glory, the emanations, the numbers, the words, in fact, the creation of God.

Jerome Rothenberg provides meditations on the alphabet in two types of poems from the collection *Poland/1931*. "Alphabet Event (1)" and "Alphabet Event (2)" are simple meditative manipulations of letters. "Word Event," which immediately follows the alphabet events, describes the ascension of the mystic as he studies the word.[16] As described by Abraham Abulafia, the meditative disciple should study the words under very particular conditions. In *Sha'erei Zadek*, the Abulafian disciple writes

> At the beginning it is advisable to decorate the house with fresh greens in order to cheer the vegetable soul which a man possesses side by side with his animal soul. Next, one should pray and sing psalms in a pleasant, melodious voice, and (read) the Torah with fervor, in order to cheer the animal soul which a man possesses side by side with his rational soul. Next, one directs his imagination to intelligible things and to understanding how one thing proceeds from another. Next, one proceeds to the moving of letters which (in their combinations) are unintelligible, thus to detach the soul (from the senses) and to cleanse it of all the forms formerly within it.[17]

The disciple proceeds to describe the skipping (*dilug*) and jumping (*kefitsah*) of idea to idea, a violent action or motion. "And if sufficient strength remains to force oneself even further and draw it out still farther, then that which is within will manifest itself without, and through the power of sheer imagination will take on the form of a polished mirror" (p. 26). In Rothenberg's "Word Event" the disciple

> sits in a house whose walls are decorated with fresh vegetables, praying & singing psalms, & reading from *The Book of Law*.

Rothenberg's disciple then turns to the movement of letters, to *dilug* and *kelfitsah*, and finally to meditation on pure abstraction, "he thinks of nothing." The initiate is "Freed from thought, the consonants dance around him in quick motion. Forming a mirror in which he sees his face." The transformation of the meditating disciple parallels precisely the transformation of the Abulafian disciple.

Numerological aspects of *kabbalistic* systems appear prominently in several of Rothenberg's "Number Events" (*Poland/1931*, pp. 75ff.), as well as in a *Notebook* entry, "11/75 (a dream)."[18] In the last, the letters appear to Rothenberg in a dream, offering the poet inspiration. The letters as part of a whole, "a solid mass against the world," nevertheless unintelligible, are a part of this apocalyptic vision. The sound of *aleph* becomes the symbol of the mystical reticence about analysis:

> "A" began it but in Hebrew not a vowel
> a choked sound it was the larynx stopped the midrash said
> > contained all sound
> sound of Alphabet initial to all speech
> as one or zero.

The letters are the foundations of creation in the dream and the basis for all numbers and all sound. Like the metrics of poetry, the numbers in *kabbalah* guide the vision. Rothenberg sees

> that I would count my way
> into the vision
> grooved thus with numbers & with sound
> the distances to every side of us
> as in a poem.

Rothenberg, like Meltzer, sees the poet and his craft as quite similar to the *kabbalist* and his study. Poetics assume cosmic significance and promise salvation or at least prediction of the messianic advent.

Other poems offer reassurance in the study of letters by describing the letters as the foundations of nature. For instance, J. Rutherford Willems, in "Hebrew Letters in the Trees," seems to promise salvation through understanding nature as a language, rationally studying creation and divinity.[19] He tries to bring mysticism into the rational realm. Two other Jewish-American poems that show the impact of Hebrew alphabet meditation on messianism and the apocalyptic most powerfully are Harvey Shapiro's "A Short History"[20] and Karl Shapiro's "The Alphabet."[21] Harvey Shapiro argues that in the modern world urbanity destroys the meaning of creation by destroying the mystery. Man forgets that "From the fiery limits of His crown/The brawling letters broke." In other words, man forgets that the creation began in destruction, and through the auspices of language, the Hebrew alphabet particularly. Only through the power, the electricity ("voltage") of language do the leaders of man ("prophet, king") assume any power or communicate any meaning. Karl Shapiro, on the other hand, distinguishes between the Hebrew alphabet (that is, Judaism) and other alphabets (that is, Gentile cultures). Hebrew letters are as "strict as flames," stubborn, "Singing through solid stone the sacred names." He compares them to barbed wire, contrasts their continuance to the lack of continuity of Roman religion, Gothic ritual, and the ovens and ghettos of Europe. Like "dancing knives," Hebrew letters can cut through darkness and the heart of man until the coming of the Messiah:

> These are the letters that all men refuse
> And will refuse until the king arrives
> And will refuse until the death of time
> And all is rolled back in the book of days.

Though the short run is given to Esau, the long run belongs to Jacob.

The most sophisticated *gematria* found as influence on contemporary Jewish-American poetry is the Abulafian variety as it appears so prominently in the poetry of Jerome Rothenberg and David Meltzer. In *A Big Jewish Book* Jerome Rothenberg describes Abulafia's mysticism as "medieval lettrism," and directs us to his idiosyncratic but successful analogue of Abulafianism with the Dadaism of Tristan Tzara and the post-World War II neo-Dadaism (that is, lettrism) of Isidore Isou.[22] Abulafia's prophetic and spiritual *kabbalah* is similar to Dadaism and lettrism only in the assertion that the unit of meaning is in the letter, not the word. Abulafia aimed meditation on the letters at the true understanding of God. Isou, and his predecessor Tzara, aimed only at the articulation of the primitive sources of human communication.

In *Abulafia's Circles*, Rothenberg aligns these disparate traditions in order to present historical precedents of his own messianic speculatons. This long poem, which unlike the poems on Abulafia discussed in Chapter 2, uses the Abulafian *kabbalah* more than the man Abulafia for symbolic structure. In three sections, Rothenberg presents three variations on the concept of Jewish Messiah. The sections center on Abraham Abulafia, Jacob Frank, and Tristan Tzara. In the concluding note to the first book publication of the poem, Rothenberg writes of the "after-images of largely unresolved messianic figures: historic & mythic" which were left after the publication of *Poland/1931* and *A Big Jewish Book*.[23] Three of these images are the figures mentioned in this series. Interweaving the historical features of the biographies of the individuals and histories of their movements, Rothenberg portrays the three as manifestations of the Messiah with the Abulafia figure as seminal, Frank and Tzara as commentary on their precedent. In the latter two sections, the Messiah legend in general, and Abraham Abulafia in particular, illuminate the individual lives of Jacob Frank and Tristan Tzara. Frank, for instance, is called "your [Abulafia's] counterpart," the one who moved toward the accomplishment of Abulafia's messianic dream (p. 78). And Tristan Tzara "dreams" Dada (p. 83) and insists that "messiahs are passee" (p. 85), but is described by Rothenberg as a "ghost of Abulafia" (p. 86).

The collection begins with the oldest of the three after-images—Abulafia—who in the first lines of the poem Rothenberg associates with revelation:

>   the master of the book
>   of lights
>   he points to them
>   & back again
>   to you
>   the letters lead his hand (p. 71).

Abraham Abulafia's creation of letters and of reality from these letters clearly indicates his messiahship. The poet mentions much of
the factual data of Abulafia's life in the section on Abulafia: the trip
to discover the mythic river Sambation and the visit to the Pope.
More important, Rothenberg makes Abulafia symbolic of almost
anarchic creativity, but the poet most forcefully contrasts Abulafian
power with the repressive and destructive power of Adolf Hitler:

o Hitler I messiah Abulafia
am bound to you
in history
where vowel calls to vowel
our paths have crossed
you kill I bring them
back to life
G-d's double nature shines thru us (p. 76).

Hitler wishes to destroy the forces of creativity and evolution in
the contemporary world, most especially Dada. Hitler says "I curse
out Dada/freaks who scrub not" (p. 75). Society identifies these
creative freaks with Rothenberg himself, as Hitler calls Rothenberg
the "false Jew" and says to him "dirty you are/needing soap" (p. 75).
Abulafia, in contrast, gives birth in Bird's Nest to a child who
transforms the Abulafian chaotic dream into "paper circles." Section
one ends

"what you hear-see
"I speak-show
"what I write
"you learn to witness
"no longer split
"no longer speech that isn't
"written on flesh (p. 78).

This passage echoes Abulafia's philosophy which synthesizes
godhead and individual and asserts that the intellect, informed by
mystic intuition, is the mode of prophecy. In his manuals of practical
kabbalah, Abulafia combines "articulation, mivta, writing, miktav,
and thought, mahshav," as the three layers of meditation.[24]

The second section of *Abulafia's Circles*, "The Secret Dream of Jacob Frank," presents Jacob Frank, the nihilist eighteenth-century convert to Catholicism, who participated in public arguments endorsing the validity of the Christian blood libel. As Abulafia's counterpart, Frank commits antinomian and offensive acts against Torah and tradition, as in the time he

> . . . mounted
> pissed 'gainst the parchment
> howling (p. 78).

Frank discovered the secrets of the faith in the "Queen of Germany," and added Christian, particularly Marian, references to his Jewish messianism. Superimposed on this heresy is the sexual license of Frank and his followers. His mistress, discussed in this second section of the poem, lives in a bordello-like apartment. The explicit sexual activity and its religious and mythic implications follow:

> "my member raised to strike
> "thee my shekinah bride
> "on eiderdowns
> "thou leans to me
> "thy mouth is like a birdcage
> "—lock me up in it!—
> "& swallow floods of love
> "like chicken drippings
> "passed from mouth to mouth
> "the tongue of me messiah Jacob Frank
> "is on the tongue of the
> "Shekinah Lilith Lady of the North (p. 80).

The image of the birdcage assumes significance for several reasons. The cage is a place of imprisonment and also safety for the bird in captivity; the female and her body function the same for the male. Her body cages his in sexual union, but it also offers him release in the sexual act and immortality in the production of children. Further, birdcage refers to Bird's Nest, the place in Jewish legend in paradise where the Messiah waits, anxiously, but studiously, until he is called to earth. In Frankist messianism, sexual union is how the Messiah waits, but the union as described here is an unproductive one, for it is *Shekinah's* mouth, not her vagina, that receives Frank's penis. Rothenberg has Frank equate the two opposing supernatural feminine forces of Jewish legend: *Shekinah* (female principle of God) and Lilith (wife of Asmodeus, therefore Queen of Hell). According to historical documents, Frank called his daughter Eva, who was his concubine, his *Shekinah*. In Frankism, therefore, the relationship between the Messiah and *Shekinah* is clearly incestuous. Rothenberg presents the female as a conflation of opposites, a source of comfort, but not of reproduction.

   Shekinah, as Queen of Heaven and as manifest in the human female, is one Frankist means of attaining salvation. The words of the songs Frank sings to his love echo combinations of the opposing feminine natures: "*la/de da*," he writes at one point in describing the music. The song Rothenberg describes variously as Italian opera, dirty songs, and songs to Torah. Later *Shekinah* assumes more similarities to Mary, and Frank's songs to *Shekinah* sound more and more like medieval lyrics in praise of the Virgin Mary. Frank says

> "my dreams are thin
> "o little g-d
> "the image of my lady floats still
> "over head
> "she sister to the sun
> "will lend a horse to me (p. 81).

Consequent to this assertion his companions become thieves, his activities gambling, drinking, and incest. The Jews speak Polish and Turkish, but the Gentiles merely look on, they

> . . . stand in awe
> sounds of entwining serpents
> in their ears (p. 82).

The evil of Frankism surrounds them, but they do not engage in it.

Moving into an urban landscape, the song of oppression of the Jews continues:

> "o the lives of Jews are hard"
> (the song goes)
> "even the messiah sits
> "in shit
> "beside the sewers   screws
> "an eye toward heaven
> lady fades
> the sun in darkness shuts
> his only lid
> box buried in the earth
> her catholic angels sing
> "hosanna"
> in the speech of mice (pp. 82–83).

In fact, the exiled position of Jews continues whatever the vagaries of the individual aspirants for messiahship, even and including those who willingly convert to Islam or Christianity.

Rothenberg concludes the poem with the eternal circle of creativity in the iconoclasm of Tristan Tzara and in cries of destruction:

> at center of a dream
> —magnetic eyes—
> whose center is a center
> & in the center
> is another center
> & in each center is a center
> & a center on each center
> centered
> centering
> composed by centers
> like earth
> the brain
> the passage to other worlds
> passage to something sad
> lost dada

an old horse rotting in the garden
maneless   waiting
for the full moon
someone leaps into the saddle
rushes after you
exuding light (p. 89).

Thus, the circle of Abulafia is passed to another. Though the last manifestation be dead as a movement, the forces of creativity and revolution continue.

Rothenberg's attraction to the nonrational traditions of Abulafia and Tzara permeate the poem, but are especially evident in the final section, "Holy Words of Tristan Tzara." Here logic becomes "complication" and "always wrong" (p. 84). Only the powerful creativity of nature itself, particularly in the form of femaleness, helps the poet create. Rothenberg alludes to numerous other twentieth-century poets and thinkers who celebrated the power of the irrational: Hannah Weiner, Osip Mandelstamm, Carl Jung, Hans Arp, and Richard Huelsenbeck. Less esoteric symbols of the irrational indicate the full measure of his syntheses: Edgar Kayce, Fritz the Kat, Bugsy Siegel, and Virginia Grey. He purposely conflates traditions and histories by acknowledging identities in names that might suggest parallels in people. For instance, in section two, "The Secret Dream of Jacob Frank," the name "Eva" suggests to him both Jacob Frank (his daughter and *Shekinah* was named Eva) and Juan Peron (his wife and protegé was named Eva). Such peculiar likenesses reenforce the attention to the sound of the name rather than to the historical data surrounding that name. Further, the sound of irrational communication (for example, the fart of Tzara) travels through Europe, to Amsterdam, to Missouri, to Brazil, and back to Rumania. Sound and its meaning travel around the world.

Completing the circle, Jerome Rothenberg himself leaps into that saddle at the end of *Abulafia's Circles*, rushes after Tristan Tzara, who is rushing after Abraham Abulafia, who in turn is rushing after the Ineffable Name of God. But for Jerome Rothenberg, the Ineffable Name of God becomes the ineffable nature of poetry, a messianic aesthetic that argues the spiritual value of abstraction in individual and idiosyncratic thought associations.

David Meltzer's "Abulafia" (discussed more fully in Chapter 2) also indicates an interest in Abraham Abulafia, but the symbolic structure is more dependent on the man Abulafia. His 1969 *Yesod*, on the other hand, depends more on the theory of Abulafianism and less on the man. *Yesod*, or foundation, the ninth *sephiroth* of God's emanation into nature, is the foundation of God's active will in the universe.[25] The title, itself, indicates Meltzer's interest in the meditative techniques of Abulafia by identifying one of the *sephira* as its title. Meditation on the ten *sephira* functioned as the preparation for the more abstract meditation on the letters in Abulafian *kabbalah*. In *Yesod*, Meltzer is quite explicit about his sources, for he adds an epigram from the *Zohar* to direct his readers and he twice refers to Abulafia by name. The epigram directs the student of meditation:

> *Happy are those who are worthy to sing song in this world! They will be found worthy to sing it again in the world to come. This hymn is built up out of 22 engraved letters and of 10 words of Creation, and all are inscribed in the Holy Name, and they are the completion and harmony of that Name.*[26]

Book II of the collection, "Yehudal: The Small Songs of Yehudi," makes several references to Abulafia as companion to the youthful singer Yehudi, who cried for the sorrows of the world and who loved with the passion of a Messiah. Yehudi's decision "to never become a poet, a scholar,/or a holy man" but rather to "become a lover" is quite in keeping with Abulafia's *kabbalah* (*Yesod*, p. 35). Abulafia writes that

> Prophecy is an intellectual matter involving the love of God, our God, the One: and it is known therefore that the lovers of prophecy are lovers of his blessed Name, and they are also blessed and beloved before the Name, and there is no doubt as to their being called wise men and prophets. Now behold and understand this: that the lovers, the loving children of prophecy, are themselves beloved: and this quality alone is the word of the blessed Name.[27]

Meltzer's Yehudi "ran with Abulafia" with whom he argued and prayed (*Yesod*, p. 36). When Yehudi disappears looking for bread, his return is awaited by his followers as is the return of the Messiah. For Meltzer, Abulafia's inspiration is to break tradition, to love and thereby to learn. The relationship between life and spirit must not be vitiated by rational, intellectual devices.

Esoteric study of language and letters and of the faces of God can become, in the Judaic tradition, a search for salvation and cosmic understanding. The meaning of the exile remains a secret, the exoteric pain and suffering of the Chosen People must symbolize something not immediately apparent. According to Lurianic *kabbalah*, the degraded presence of God in creation explains the present exile. The contemporary poet sees in this tradition an interpretation of man's place in the universe. Susan Mernit believes a new age is on us; John Hollander sees only a spectrum of repetition. According to the Abulafian mode of apocalyptic messianism only through meditative techniques that direct the individual to the true nature of God can understanding or salvation be attained. The poetic, modern interpretation of that tradition allows poets to direct their attention carefully to the form of language, the looks of words, while at the same time asking questions of substance. Jack Hirschman most clearly works within this Hebraic tradition of letter and word study in order to raise significant contemporary moral and political questions. His poems on Jerusalem, for instance, while referring to the biblical and Blakean traditions of the home of Judaism are also weeping over the American crimes in Viet Nam. Jerome Rothenberg searches in the mystery of language and numbers for a poetic inspiration that will allow him to celebrate his idiosyncratic vision of human existence that conflates all religions, cultures, historical eras, and disciplines. If there is a truth behind language, an abstract and absolute truth, then it must fund the meaning for all existence in all cultures, at all times, and in all modes. Finding that answer will indeed produce the Messiah, understanding. David Meltzer quite consciously stays within a traditional Jewish philosophy and further exemplifies Harold Bloom's sense of the anxiety of influence when in "Abulafia," he writes:

"Abulafia, dont kid me." And Abulafia would never kid a kidder, for the power of Hebraic language study and emanation theory and their promise in Judaism continues in contemporary Jewish-American poetry. The symbolic structure derived from apocalyptic messianism apparent in these last poems discussed provides a mystical structure. The cosmic consequences of such a structure indicate both the depth and the seriousness of the *kabbalistic* influence here. Whether the symbolic structure supports a poem of sociological criticism, of aesthetic commentary, or of philosophical vision, these poems are written by authors for whom apocalyptic symbols express an ancient attitude toward man's place in the universe and his relationship toward God.

Conclusion

Perhaps we can best understand the apocalyptic influence on contemporary Jewish-American poetry if we place that poetry within another broad context: the gradual confrontation of the Holocaust by American Jews. This confrontation is quite a recent phenomenon. Literary and social historians have identified two events as the benchmarks of this new American consciousness: the trial of Adolf Eichmann in 1962 and the Six-Day War of Israel in 1967.[1] However, the literary critics have been skeptical of American Holocaust literature. In the several excellent critical commentaries on the impact of the Holocaust on contemporary Jewish poetry, these writers either overlook the American artist in their discussions or look with disdain on his treatment as inauthentic.[2] This avoidance of commenting on the American artist partially results from these critics' natural affinity for European over American literature, but also results from a demand for facticity infused with personal experience, a belief that the horror of the Holocaust must be written of in experiential literature. Such a requirement both confines the possibility of that era as a source for aesthetic response and denies the possibility of there ever being an American response. One of these critics, Sidra Dekoven Ezrahi, presents what seems to me to be a much more fertile evaluation of the Jewish-American version of the Holocaust. She argues that the historical remove of the twenty years from 1944 to 1964, from the end of the Holocaust to the appearance of the Holocaust as a subject in Jewish-American letters, should not be a point of criticism. Rather, she sees the remove as the "basic existential premise," both "the boundary and the resource as well as the ultimate challenge for the imagination."[3] Within this context, I find two general modes of response to the Holocaust in American letters. One makes specific reference to the facts and features of the historical era of the Nazi final solution, either placing that event on a continuum of other pogroms (for example, Anthony Hecht, *Rites and Ceremonies*)[4] or suggesting its singularity by imagination's power (such as, Irving Feldman, "Pripet Marshes")[5] or the objective facts of the case at hand (for example, Charles Reznikoff, *Holocaust*).[6] In other words, this poetry uses literal reference to a specific catastrophe, an event on which the apocalyptic genre is most often based. The other mode uses apocalyptic themes, modes, and symbols without specific reference to the specific historical event or indeed to its typological counterpart, the apocalypse (the poetry and prose discussed in the previous chapters of this book).

None of these American poets tries to confront the Holocaust as European survivors would, but do so as Americans and as American Jews. They studied Whitman and viewed death-camp snapshots; they inhabit Anthony Hecht's "wilderness of comfort," and therefore they suffer a particular kind of survivor guilt. In America, Jews know that they have never endured the horrors of European anti-Semitism. But Jews also know that most Americans are non-Jews of European descent, and the fear of, shall we say, the racial memory for this anti-Semitism is strong. The Jews have, after all, lived in America only three centuries and been a significant minority here for barely one century; they lived in Europe for almost two millenia. In this perspective, even American Jews become survivors of the Holocaust. Thereby, Jews know better than any American group the important truth of George Santayana's threat of the consequences of forgetting the past. And so these Jewish-American poets remember and protest.

The three poems cited in this section that specifically refer to the historical event of the Holocaust suggest the very same concern with language that we have noted throughout our analysis of the

poetry influenced by the Jewish apocalyptic. Charles Reznikoff in
Holocaust tries to approach the event by the objective mode, indicating the only way to the truth of the happening is through
presentation of the most facts that are verifiable by historical
documents. His form, the twelve books of his poem, suggest the
epic proportions of the event, with the epic hero being the Jewish
People and the epic act—survival. Hecht's *Rites and Ceremonies*, a
more symbolic confrontation with the Holocaust, concludes on a
religious note, with a plea for Jews to feel Christian charity for the
anti-Semites. Feldman's "Pripet Marshes," ostensibly the most personal because of his specific reference to his own acquaintances,
becomes the most universal evaluation of the Holocaust for the
Jewish American, because Feldman so clearly bases his poem on the
existential premise of historical and geographical separation of
America from the Nazi Holocaust. His poem suggests that silence
itself is not a failure to confront an issue; silence can be a statement
too. The linguistic possibilities then become nonevaluative citation
of detail, liturgical requests for charity, and silence.

The major theoreticians of Holocaust literature recognize the
problem of language and its relationship to imagination and creativity. The problem of how to say it becomes the essential question in
this body of literature. Even in the wilderness of comfort that is
America, these concerns of language appear. These American Jews
believe that the Holocaust has transformed the spirit of man; it has
made us revise our expectations, transformed our words and our art,
in whatever language we speak, in whatever country we live. Most
American-Jewish poets, however, unlike their European or Yiddish-
speaking coreligionists have not cited the specifics of the Nazi final
solution, rather they have reverted to the most traditional Jewish
mode of confronting catastrophe: the Jewish apocalyptic. With
Daniel and Enoch, Abulafia and Luria, the contemporary Jewish-
Americans have written poetry of esoteric form and powerful intent.
With Daniel they bemoan their failure to understand the meanings
of history and visions, but with Daniel they seem to be willing to
wait and follow God's directions to the earlier apocalyptist: "[G]o
thou thy way till the end be; and thou shalt rest, and shalt stand up
to thy lot, at the end of the days" (Daniel, 12:13).

Notes

Introduction

1. Harold Bloom, *Figures of Capable Imagination* (New York: A Continuum Book, The Seabury Press, 1976), 247.

2. Ibid., 260. This combination is apparent in most of the poems discussed in my text.

3. Though Ada Isaacs Menken (c. 1835–1868) also wrote verse during this period, she is better remembered for her flamboyant life style than for her poetry.

4. Stephen Birmingham, *The Grandees* (New York: Harper & Row, 1971) discusses this Sephardic group.

5. *Union Hymnal: Songs and Prayers for Jewish Worship*, 3rd ed. (New York: Central Conference of American Rabbis, 1954), 168.

6. "The New Colossus," is one of the most often anthologized poems in collections of Jewish-American literature, in *The Poems of Emma Lazarus*, vol. I (Boston: Houghton, Mifflin and Company, 1889), 202.

7. Charles Reznikoff, "Glosses," in *A Short History of Israel, Poems 1937-1976*, vol. II of the *Complete Poems* (Santa Barbara, Ca.: Black Sparrow Press, 1976), 22.

8. Ibid., 22–23.

9. Ibid., 120–121.

10. Ibid., 121.

11. Hyam Plutzik, "For T. S. E. Only," in *Apples From Shinar* (Middletown, Conn.: Wesleyan University Press, 1959), 28–29.

12. Howard Schwartz, "Introduction to Book III: United States," in *Voices Within the Ark: The Modern Jewish Poets* (New York: Pushcart Press, 1980), 378–390, gives an interesting overview of the poetry in America, particularly useful in the listing of contemporary poetry. He describes the poets by generations, in terms of birth dates: those born at the end of the nineteenth century (for example, Reznikoff), those born in the 1910s (for example, Karl Shapiro), and those born between 1920 and 1935 (such as, Philip Levine and Allen Ginsberg and his California mystical associates), and gives a list of contemporaries especially influenced by Jewish groups (for example, Marcia Falk and the Boston Havurah movement).

13. Bernard Martin, Introduction to *Movements and Issues in American Judaism: An Analysis and Sourcebook of Developments Since 1945* (Westport, Conn.: Greenwood Press, 1978).

14. See entry on John Hollander in James Vinson's *Contemporary Poets* (London: St. Martin's Press, 1980).

15. Richard Jackson, "John Hollander, 1978: The Candle in the Pitcher," in *Acts of Mind: Conversations with Contemporary Poets* (Tuscaloosa: University of Alabama Press, 1983), 197, 198, 204.

16. Jerome Rothenberg, "A Dialogue on Oral Poetry," and "Pre-Face to a Symposium on Ethnopoetics, in *Pre-Faces and Other Writings* (New York: A New Directions Book, 1981), 9–47, 129–136.

17. Jerome Rothenberg, "Preface," *Symposium of the Whole: A Range of Discourse Toward an Ethnopoetics* (Berkeley: University of California Press, 1983), xi note.

18. Muriel Rukeyser, "To Be a Jew in the Twentieth Century," section V of "Letter to the Front," in *The Collected Poems* (New York: McGraw-Hill, 1978), 239.

Chapter 1. Definitions and Historical Context

1. Gershom Scholem, "The Messianic Idea in Kabbalism," in *The*

Messianic Idea in Judaism and Other Essays on Jewish Spirituality (New York: Schocken Books, 1971), 37–39.

2. Stephen Sharot, *Messianism, Mysticism, and Magic: A Sociological Analysis of Jewish Religious Movements* (Chapel Hill: University of North Carolina Press, 1982), 62.

3. David G. Roskies, *Against the Apocalypse: Responses to Catastrophe in Modern Jewish Culture* (Cambridge: Harvard University Press, 1984), 9.

4. Ibid., 225.

5. According to Roskies, except for the use of Christ and crucifixion images (see Roskies's chapter 10) and a couple of instances in M. L. Halpern, "A Night," L. Shapiro, "White Chalah," and Pietro Rawicz, *Blood From the Sky*, apocalypticism is not significant for these artists.

6. In fact, Roskies spends very little time discussing the apocalyptic genre, indeed not even using the usual generic term for the tradition. The classical texts of Jewish apocalyptic seem to be unimportant to the analysis: he never mentions the literature Enoch, and the Book of Daniel is cited only four times in a three-hundred-page book.

7. Hayden White, "The Historical Text as Literary Artifact," in *The Writing of History: Literary Form and Historical Understanding*, edited by Robert H. Canary and Henry Kozicki (Madison: The University of Wisconsin Press, 1978), 54.

8. Raphael Patai, *The Messiah Texts* (Detroit: Wayne State University Press, 1979), xv.

9. Frank Kermode, *The Sense of an Ending: Studies in the Theory of Fiction* (New York: Oxford University Press, 1967), 3–31, 93.

10. D. H. Lawrence, *Apocalypse and the Writings on Revelation*, edited by Mara Kalnes (Cambridge: Cambridge University Press, 1980), 80.

11. Stanley Brice Frost, *Old Testament Apocalyptic: Its Origins and Growth* (London: The Epworth Press, 1952), 32–34.

12. Ibid., 42.

13. Ibid., 57–66.

14. Ibid., 67.

15. Ibid.

16. Stanley Brice Frost, "Apocalyptic and History," in *The Bible in Modern Scholarship*, edited by J. Philip Hyatt (Nashville and New York: Abingdon Press, 1965), 99, 105.

17. Joshua Bloch, *On the Apocalyptic in Judaism*, Jewish Quarterly *Review* Monograph Series, Number II (Philadelphia: Dropsie College, 1952), 17, note 35.

18. Frost, *Old Testament Apocalyptic*, 4.

19. D. S. Russell, *The Method and Message of Jewish Apocalyptic: 200 BC–AD 100* (London: SCM Press, Ltd., 1964), 205–206.

20. Ibid., 105.

21. See D. S. Russell's account of Lindbloom's definition of apocalyptic, Ibid.

22. Frost, *Old Testament Apocalyptic*, 129.

23. John R. May, *Toward a New Earth: Apocalypse in the American Novel* (Notre Dame: University of Notre Dame, 1972), 13.

24. Bloch, *On the Apocalyptic*, 48.

25. Ibid., 49.

26. Ibid., 49–51.

27. Ibid., 49.

28. Joseph Sarachek, *The Doctrine of the Messiah in Medieval Jewish Literature* (New York: Jewish Theological Seminary of America, 1932), 9–10.

29. Abba Hillel Silver, *A History of Messianic Speculation in Israel: From the First through the Seventeenth Centuries* (New York: The Macmillan Company, 1927), xi.

30. Book of Daniel in the *Holy Scriptures* (Philadelphia: Jewish Publication Society of America, 1959), 1018.

31. *Pirke de Rabbi Eliezer: (The Chapters of Rabbi Eliezer the Great) According to the Text of the Manuscript Belonging to Abraham Epstein of Vienna*, translated and annotated by Gerald Friedlander (New York: Hermon Press, 1970).

32. Book of Enoch, in Volume II, *The Apocrypha and Pseudoepigrapha*

of the Old Testament in English, edited by R. H. Charles (Oxford: The Clarendon Press, 1978), 163–281.

33. A major Yiddish-American poet, Aaron Zeitlin, wrote a poem, *Metatron*, which appeared in an early edition in 1921, but was considerably revised for a 1957, post-Holocaust edition. The apocalyptic message of Enoch permeates the poem.

34. Abraham Abulafia, "*Sha'rei Zedek*," in *The Path of the Names: Writings by Abraham ben Samuel Abulafia*, edited by David Meltzer (London: Trigram, Tree, 1976), 21.

35. Abulafia, "Selections from *Haye Olam Ha-Ba*," in *The Path of the Names*, 39–40.

36. Abulafia, "*Sefer Ha-Ot*," in *The Path of the Names*, 41–73.

37. Jerome Rothenberg, with Harris Lenowitz and Charles Doria (eds.), *A Big Jewish Book* (Garden City, N.Y.: Anchor Press, 1978), 405–406.

38. David Meltzer (ed.), *The Secret Garden: An Anthology in the Kabbalah* (New York: A Continuum Book, The Seabury Press, 1975), xiii–xiv.

39. Gershom G. Scholem, *Major Trends in Jewish Mysticism* (New York: Schocken Books, 1972), 244.

40. See for instance, David Meltzer (ed.), Part Seven, in *The Secret Garden*, 171–214; various excerpts in Jerome Rothenberg with Harris Lenowitz and Charles Doria (eds.), *A Big Jewish Book*; and *Tales in Praise of the Ari*, translated by Aaron Klein and Jenny Machlowitz Klein (Philadelphia: Jewish Publication Society of America, 1970).

41. Scholem, *Major Trends*, 275.

42. Ibid., 286.

43. The novelistic renditions of these messianic aspirants and others will be discussed in the second chapter.

44. Gershom Scholem, *Sabbatai Sevi: The Mystical Messiah, 1626-1676*, Bollingen Series XCIII (Princeton: Princeton University Press, 1973).

45. See Harris Lenowitz and Dan Chopyk, "Fifty Sayings of the Lord Jacob Frank," *Alcheringa: Ethnopoetics* 3 (1977), 32–51; and Jerome Rothenberg, *A Big Jewish Book*, 321–328.

46. See for instance selections in *A Big Jewish Book*; and David Meltzer (ed.), Part Eight, in *The Secret Garden*, 215–227.

47. Holocaust scholars suggest that the two most important events in bringing the European horror into the American consciousness were the Eichmann trial and the Six-Day War (see for instance, Sidra DeKoven Ezrahi, *By Words Alone: The Holocaust in Literature* [Chicago: The University of Chicago Press, 1982], 205ff.).

Chapter 2. Apocalyptic Historiography and the Messianic Hopeful

1. John Milfull, "The Messiah and the Direction of History: Walter Benjamin, Isaac Bashevis Singer and Franz Kafka," in *Festschrift for E. W. Herd*, edited by August Obermayer, Otago German Studies, vol. I (Dunedin, New Zealand: Department of German, University of Otago, 1980), 150.

2. Gershom Scholem, "Toward an Understanding of the Messianic Idea in Judaism," in *Messianic Idea in Judaism and Other Essays on Jewish Spirituality* (New York: Schocken Books, 1971), 4.

3. David Biale, *Gershom Scholem: Kabbalah and Counter-History* (Cambridge, Ma.: Harvard University Press, 1979), 164–165.

4. Gershom Scholem, "Toward an Understanding," 35.

5. Biale, *Gershom Scholem*, 195.

6. Georg Lukacs, *The Historical Novel*, trans. by Hannah and Stanley Mitchell (New York: Humanities Press, 1965), 43, 58.

7. Victor Lange, "Fact in Fiction," *Comparative Literature Studies* 6 (1969), 261.

8. Ursula Brumm, "Thoughts on History and the Novel," *Comparative Literature Studies* 6 (1969), 324.

9. Leon Feuchtwanger, *The House of Desdemona; or, The Laurels and Limitations of Historical Fiction*, trans. by Harold A. Basilius (Detroit: Wayne State University, 1963), 129.

10. Irving Feldman, "The Apocalypse is a School for Prophets," in *Lost Originals: Poems* (Chicago: Holt, Rinehart and Winston, 1972), 36–37.

11. Myra Sklarew, "Instructions for the Messiah," in *Voices within the Ark: The Modern Jewish Poets*, edited by Howard Schwartz and Anthony Rudolf (New York: The Pushcart Press, 1980), 660–661.

12. Arthur A. Cohen, *In the Days of Simon Stern* (New York: Random House, 1973), 140.

13. Rose Drachler, "Athens and Jerusalem," in *The Collected Poems* (New York: Assembling Press, 1983), 118.

14. Edouard Roditi, "The Messiah Ben Joseph," in *Thrice Chosen* (Santa Barbara: Black Sparrow Press, 1981), 25.

15. Abraham Abulafia, "Selections from *Haye Olam Ha-Ba*," in *The Path of the Names: Writings by Abraham ben Samuel Abulafia*, edited by David Meltzer (London: Trigram, Tree, 1976), 39.

16. David Meltzer, *Yesod* (London: Trigram Press, 1969), 26.

17. Gershom Scholem, *Major Trends in Jewish Mysticism*, 3rd rev. ed. (New York: Schocken Press, 1972), 131.

18. Ibid., 141.

19. Jack Hirschman, "Eluardian Elohenu for Allen Ginsberg," in *Black Alephs, Poems 1960-1968* (London: Trigram Press, 1969), 123.

20. Jack Hirschman, "Hymn," in *Black Alephs*, 40–41.

21. Jerome Rothenberg, "History Seven," in *Poland/1931* (New York: New Directions, 1974), 137.

22. Harry Simonhoff, *The Chosen One* (London: Thomas Yoseloff, 1964), 597–598.

23. Jack Hirschman, "The R of the Ari's Raziel" (Los Angeles: The Press of the Pegacycle Lady, 1972), np, and Jack Hirschman, "The Ari," in *Black Alephs*, 118–121.

24. Jack Hirschman (trans.), Jacob Tausk of Prague's "Ein Schon Neu Lied fun Moschiach," in *The Secret Garden: An Anthology in the Kabbalah*, edited by David Meltzer (New York: A Continuum Book, The Seabury Press, 1976), 223–227.

25. Jerome Rothenberg (trans.), "4 Poems for Sabbatai Zevi," in *A Big Jewish Book: Poems & Other Visions of the Jews from Tribal Times to Present*, edited by Jerome Rothenberg with Harris Lenowitz and Charles Doria (Garden City, N.Y.: Anchor Press, 1978), 314–316.

26. Leonard Wolf, *The False Messiah* (Boston: Houghton Mifflin Co., 1982), 277.

27. John Hollander, "The Loss of Smyrna," in *Spectral Emanations: New and Selected Poems* (New York: Atheneum, 1978), 95.

28. Jerome Rothenberg, "Satan in Goray: A Homage to Isaac Bashevis Singer," in *Poland/1931*, 7–9.

Chapter 3. Allegory and the Messianic Story

1. Rose Drachler, "The Prophet," in *The Collected Poems of Rose Drachler* (New York: Assembling Press, 1983), 103.

2. Rose Drachler, "The Witness," in *The Collected Poems*, 104.

3. Harvey Shapiro, "The Prophet Announces," in *Battle Report: Selected Poems* (Middletown, Conn.: Wesleyan University Press, 1966), 46.

4. Irving Feldman, "The Messengers," in *Pripet Marshes and Other Poems* (New York: Viking, 1965), 32.

5. Howard Schwartz, "Our Angels," in *Gathering the Sparks: Poems 1965–1979* (St. Louis: Singing Wind Press, 1979), 57.

6. David Meltzer, *Tens: Selected Poems, 1961–1971* (New York: McGraw-Hill Book Company, 1973), 116–125.

7. Raphael Patai, *The Hebrew Goddess* (Philadelphia: KTAV Publishing House, 1976), 143.

8. Ibid., 143, 145.

9. Jack Hirschman, "Ari," in *Black Alephs: Poems 1960–1968* (London: Trigram Press, 1969), 118–121.

10. Howard Schwartz, "Song of Ascent," in *Gathering*, 11; "Neshamah," in *Gathering*, 14; "The Robe of the Shekhina," in *Gathering*, 24–25.

11. Jack Hirschman, "El," in *Black Alephs*, 33.

12. Jack Hirschman, "Holy Kabbalah," in *Black Alephs*, 146.

13. Jack Hirschman, "Zohara," in *Black Alephs*, 117.

14. Edouard Roditi, "Shekhina and the Kiddushim," in *Voices Within*

the Ark: The Modern Jewish Poets, edited by Howard Schwartz and Anthony Rudolf (New York: Pushcart Press, 1980), 601–602.

15. Jack Hirschman, "There is a Beautiful Maiden Who Has No Eyes Who is the True Messiah," in *A Big Jewish Book: Poems & Visons of the Jews from Tribal Times to Present*, edited by Jerome Rothenberg with Harris Lenowitz and Charles Doria (Garden City, N.Y.: Anchor Press, Doubleday, 1978), 37–38.

16. Jerome Rothenberg, "She," in *Poland/1931* (New York: New Directions, 1974), 79–80.

17. Jerome Rothenberg, "Poland/1931: The Bride," in *Poland/1931*, 26.

18. Jerome Rothenberg, "9/75: A Letter to Nathaniel Tarn to Honor *Lyrics for the Bride of God*," in *The Notebooks* (Milwaukee, Wis.: The Membrane Press, 1976), 9.

19. Jerome Rothenberg, "Galician Nights, or A Novel in Progress," in *Poland/1931*, 82.

20. Jerome Rothenberg, "Esther K. Comes to America," in *Poland/1931*, 109.

21. Jerome Rothenberg, "Isaac Luria's 'Hymn to Shekinah for the Feast of Sabbath' Newly Set Rosh Hashonah 5733 by Jerome Rothenberg," in *Poland/1931*, 97.

22. Jerome Rothenberg, "History One," in *Poland/1931*, 123.

23. Donald Finkel, "Lilith," in *Voices Within the Ark*, 460–461.

24. Jascha Kessler, "Waiting for Lilith," in *Voices Within the Ark*, 499.

25. Howard Schwartz, "Lilith," in *Gathering*, 74.

26. Ruth Feldman, "Lilith," in *Voices Within the Ark*, 459.

27. Allen Grossman, "Lilith," in *Voices Within the Ark*, 480.

28. Jerome Rothenberg, "10/75: A Letter to Meltzer for His Third Visit to Milwaukee," in *The Notebooks*, 17.

29. David Meltzer, "Lil," in *Hero/Lil* (Los Angeles: Black Sparrow Press, 1973), 33–86.

30. Howard Schwartz, "Gathering the Sparks," in *Gathering*, 16–17.

31. David Meltzer, *A Midrash*, in *Tens*, 141.

32. Anthony Hecht, "Exile," in *Millions of Strange Shadows* (New York: Atheneum, 1977), 45.

33. Irving Feldman, *Works and Days*, in *Works and Days and Other Poems* (Boston: An Atlantic Monthly Press Book, Little, Brown and Company, 1961), 33–51.

34. Robert Mezey, *The Wandering Jew*, in *The Lovemaker* (Iowa City: The Cummington Press, 1961), 55–71. *The Wandering Jew* collects several poems, including "Against Seasons," "With My God the Smith," and "Wandering Jew."

35. Irving Feldman, "The Wandering Jew," in *Works and Days*, 94–101.

Chapter 4. The Messianic Ontology

1. See chapter one for a fuller explanation of these theories.

2. Susan Mernit, *The Angelic Alphabet*, in *The Angelic Alphabet* (Berkeley: Tree, 1975), np. this collection of poems is divided into two sections: "Aleph" and "Beth." "Aleph" contains seven poems, the last of which is the twelve-section poem under discussion.

3. John Hollander, *Spectral Emanations*, in *Spectral Emanations: New and Selected Poems* (New York: Atheneum, 1978), 3.

4. *Jewish Encyclopedia*, vol. 18, 494.

5. Harold Bloom, Review of *Spectral Emanations*, *New Republic* 179 (September 9, 1978), 42.

6. Harold Bloom, "The White Light of Trope: An Essay on John Hollander's '*Spectral Emanations*,'" *Kenyon Review* NS 1 (Winter 1979), 102.

7. Ibid., 105, suggests that the narrator is departed indigo, all other names representing the colors of the poem, such as Gelb (yellow in German), Krasny (red in Russian), and Pomaranczowy (orange in Polish).

8. There are even several Jewish poets who write symbolic books on the English alphabet: such as Susan Fromberg Schaeffer, *Alphabet for the Lost Years* (1976). This book is influenced by the same sense of mystical

information invested in the Hebrew language as is apparent in Laurence Kushner, *The Book of Letters* (1975), Stuart A. Perkoff, *alphabet* (1973), and Rose Drachler, "The Letters of the Book" (1977).

9. Jerome Rothenberg, "*Aleph* Poem," in *Vienna Blood and Other Poems* (New York: New Directions, 1980), 59 and "A Poem for *Ayin*," in *Vienna Blood*, 64.

10. Harvey Shapiro, "Aleph," in *Battle Report: Selected Poems* (Middletown, Conn.: Wesleyan University Press, 1967), 52.

11. Harvey Shapiro, "The Six Hundred Thousand Letters," in *Battle Report*, 39.

12. Emily Borenstein, "Life of the Letters," in *Voices Within the Ark: The Modern Jewish Poets*, edited by Howard Schwartz and Anthony Rudolf (New York: Pushcart Press, 1980), 427.

13. David Meltzer, "Letters & Numbers," in *Tens: Selected Poems, 1961-1971* (New York: McGraw-Hill Book Company, 1973), 109.

14. Jack Hirschman, "Fingerpoint," in *Black Alephs, Poems 1960-1968* (London: Trigram Press, 1969), 36.

15. Jack Hirschman, "Ascent," in *Black Alephs*, 35–36.

16. Jerome Rothenberg, "Alphabet Event (1)," "Alphabet Event (2)," and "Word Event," in *Poland/1931* (New York: New Directions, 1974), 72–73.

17. Abraham Abulafia, "*Sha'rei Zedek*," in *The Path of the Names: Writings by Abraham ben Samuel Abulafia*, edited by David Meltzer (London: Trigram, Tree, 1976), 25–26.

18. Jerome Rothenberg, "11/75: (a dream)," in *The Notebooks* (Milwaukee, Wis.: The Membrane Press, 1976), 72–73.

19. J. Rutherford Willems, "Hebrew Letters in the Trees," in *Voices Within the Ark*, 672–673.

20. Harvey Shapiro, "A Short History," in *Battle Report*, 54.

21. Karl Shapiro, "The Alphabet," in *Poems of a Jew* (New York: Random House, 1958), 3.

22. Jerome Rothenberg with Harris Lenowitz and Charles Doria, *A Big Jewish Book: Poems & Other Visions of the Jews from Tribal Times to Present* (Garden City, N.Y.: Anchor Press, Doubleday, 1978), 405.

23. Jerome Rothenberg, *Abulafia's Circles*, in *Vienna Blood*, 89–90.

24. Gershom Scholem, *Major Trends in Jewish Mysticism*, 3rd rev. ed. (New York: Schocken Press, 1972), 135.

25. The *sephira* of God are God's aspects in the cosmos. The theory is much more pertinent to Lurianic *kabbalah* than to any other *kabbalah* discussed in this book.

26. David Meltzer, *Yesod* (London: Trigram Press, 1969), title page.

27. Abulafia, "The Question of Prophecy," in *The Path of the Names*, 31.

Conclusion

1. Edward Alexander, *Resonance of Dust: Essays on Holocaust Literature and Jewish Fate* (Columbus: Ohio State University Press, 1979), 127.

2. These books include Edward Alexander's (see note 1); Sidra DeKoven Ezrahi, *By Words Alone: The Holocaust in Literature* (Chicago: University of Chicago Press, 1980); Alvin Rosenfeld, *A Double Dying: Reflections on Holocaust Literature* (Bloomington: Indiana University Press, 1980); Alvin H. Rosenfeld and Irving Greenberg (eds.), *Confronting the Holocaust: The Impact of Elie Wiesel* (Bloomington: Indiana University Press, 1978); and Lawrence L. Langer, *The Holocaust and the Literary Imagination* (New Haven: Yale University Press, 1975).

3. Ezrahi, *By Words Alone*, 180.

4. Anthony Hecht, "*Rites and Ceremonies*," in *The Hard Hours* (New York: Atheneum, 1967), 38–47.

5. Irving Feldman, "Pripet Marshes," in *Pripet Marshes and Other Poems* (New York: Viking, 1965), 44–47.

6. Charles Reznikoff, *Holocaust* (Santa Barbara: Black Sparrow Press, 1975).

Bibliography

Apocalyptic and Messianic Texts

The Anchor Bible: Book of Daniel. Introduction by Louis F. Hartman and Alexander A. DiLella. New York: Doubleday, 1977.

Charles, R.H., ed. *The Apocrypha and Pseudoepigrapha of the Old Testament in English.* 2 vols. Oxford: The Clarendon Press, 1913. Reprint, 1978.

Jacobs, Louis, ed. *Jewish Mystical Testimonies.* New York: Schocken Books, 1977.

Lenowitz, Harris, and Dan Chopyk. "Fifty Sayings of the Lord Jacob Frank." *Alcheringa/Ethnopoetics* 3: 2 (1977), 32–54.

Meltzer, David, ed. *The Path of the Names: Writings by Abraham ben Samuel Abulafia.* London: Trigram, Tree, 1976.

———, ed. *The Secret Garden: An Anthology in the Kabbalah.* New York: A Continuum Book, The Seabury Press, 1976.

Patai, Raphael, ed. *The Messiah Texts.* Detroit: Wayne State University Press, 1979.

Pirke de Rabbi Eliezer: (The Chapters of Rabbi Eliezer the Great) According to the Text of the Manuscript Belonging to Abraham Epstein of Vienna. Translated by Gerald Friedlander. London: 1916. Reprint, New York: Herman Press, 1970.

Tales in Praise of the Ari. Translated from the Hebrew by Aaron Klein and Jenny Machlowitz Klein. Philadelphia: Jewish Publication Society of America, 1970.

Primary Literary Texts

Cohen, Arthur A. *In the Days of Simon Stern*. New York: Random House, 1973.

Drachler, Rose. *Burrowing In, Digging Out*. Berkeley: Tree, 1974.

———. *The Choice*. Berkeley: Tree, 1977.

———. *The Collected Poems*. New York: Assembling Press, 1983.

Feldman, Irving. *Lost Originals*. Chicago: Holt, Rinehart and Winston, 1972.

———. *Magic Papers and Other Poems*. New York: Harper and Row, Publishers, 1970.

———. *Preipet Marshes and Other Poems*. New York: Viking, 1965.

———. *Works and Days and Other Poems*. Boston: An Atlantic Monthly Press Book, Little, Brown and Company, 1961.

Fiedler, Leslie A. *The Messengers Will Come No More*. New York: Stein and Day, 1974.

Gavron, Daniel. *The End of Days*. Philadelphia: Jewish Publication Society of America, 1970.

Gilner, Elias. *Prince of Israel: A Novel on Bar-Kokba's Uprising Against Rome*. New York: Exposition Press, 1952.

Hecht, Anthony. *The Hard Hours*. New York: Atheneum, 1968.

———. *Millions of Strange Shadows*. New York: Atheneum, 1977.

Hollander, John. *Spectral Emanations: New and Selected Poems*. New York: Atheneum, 1978.

Hirschman, Jack. *Black Alephs: Poems 1960-1968*. London: Trigram Press, 1969.

———.*The R of the Ari's Raziel*. Los Angeles: The Press of the Pegacycle Lady, 1972.

Mandel, Arthur. *The Militant Messiah or the Flight from the Ghetto. The Story of Jacob Frank and the Frankist Movement*. Atlantic Highlands, N.J.: Humanities Press, Scholarly Books, 1979.

Martin, Bernard. *That Man from Smyrna: An Historical Novel*. Middle Village, N.Y.: Jonathan David Publishers, 1978.

Meisels, Andrew. *Son of a Star*. New York: G. P. Putnam's Sons, 1969.

Meltzer, David. *Hero/Lil*. Los Angeles: Black Sparrow Press, 1973.

———. *Tens: Selected Poems, 1961-1971*. New York: McGraw-Hill Book Company, 1973.

———. *Yesod*. London: Trigram Press, 1969.

Mernit, Susan. *The Angelic Alphabet*. Berkeley: Tree, 1975.

Mezey, Robert. *The Lovemaker*. Iowa City, Ia.: The Cummington Press, 1961.

————. *The Wandering Jew*. Mount Vernon, Ia.: The Hillside Press, 1960.

Perkoff, Stuart Z. *alphabet*. Los Angeles: The Red Hill Press, 1973.

Reznikoff, Charles. *The Complete Poems*. Vols. I and II by Seamus Cooney. Santa Barbara: Black Sparrow Press, 1976.

————. *Holocaust*, Santa Barbara: Black Sparrow Press, 1975.

Roditi, Edouard. *Thrice Chosen*. Santa Barbara: Black Sparrow Press, 1981.

Rosenfeld, Isaac. *Alpha and Omega*. New York: The Viking Press, 1966.

Rothenberg, Jerome. *The Notebooks*. Milwaukee, Wis.: Membrane Press, 1976.

————. *Poland/1931*. New York: A New Directions Book, 1974.

————. *Vienna Blood and Other Poems*. New York: A New Directions Book, 1980.

———— with Harris Lenowitz and Charles Doria. *A Big Jewish Book: Poems & Other Visions of the Jews from Tribal Times to the Present*. Garden City, N.Y.: Anchor Press, Doubleday, 1978.

Samuel, Maurice. *The Second Crucifixion*. New York: Alfred A. Knopf, 1960.

Schwartz, Howard. *Blessing Over Ashes*. Berkeley: Tree, 1974.

————. *The Captive Soul of the Messiah*. St. Louis: The Cauldron Press, 1979.

————. *Gathering the Sparks: Poems 1965-1979*. St. Louis, Mo.: Singing Wind Press, 1979.

————. *Lilith's Cave*. San Francisco: Isthmus Press, 1975.

———— and Anthony Rudolf, eds. *Voices Within the Ark: The Modern Jewish Poets*. Yonkers, N.Y.: The Pushcart Press, 1980.

Shapiro, Harvey. *Battle Report: Selected Poems*. Middletown, Conn.: Wesleyan University Press, 1966.

Shapiro, Karl. *Poems of a Jew*. New York: Random House, 1958.

Simonhoff, Harry. *The Chosen One*. New York: Thomas Yoseloff, 1964.

Wolf, Leonard. *False Messiah*. Boston: Houghton Mifflin Co., 1982.

Zeldis, Chayyim. *Brothers*. New York: Random House, 1976.

Zukerman, William. *Refugee from Judea and Other Jewish Tales*. New York: Philosophical Library, 1964.

Secondary Sources

Alexander, Edward. *Resonance of Dust: Essays on Holocaust Literature and Jewish Fate*. Columbus: Ohio State University Press, 1979.

Altieri, Charles. "Sensibility, Rhetoric, and Will: Some Tensions in Contemporary Poetry." *Contemporary Literature* 23: 4 (1982), 452–479.

Anderson, G. W. *Tradition and Interpretation*. Oxford: Clarendon Press, 1979.

Baumgarten, Murray. "The Historical Novel: Some Postulates." *Clio* 4: 2 (1975), 173–182.

Berger, Abraham. "The Messianic Self-Consciousness of Abraham Abulafia: A Tentative Evaluation." In *Essays on Jewish Life and Thought: Presented in Honor of Salo Wittmayer Baron*. Edited by Joseph L. Blau, Arthur Hertzberg, Philip Friedman, and Isaac Mendelsohn. New York: Columbia University Press, 1959, 55–61.

Berthoff, Warner. "Fiction, History, Myth: Notes Toward the Discrimination of Narrative Forms." In *The Interpretation of Narrative: Theory and Practice*. Harvard English Studies #1. Edited by Morton W. Bloomfield. Cambridge: Harvard University Press, 1970, 263–287.

Biale, David. *Gershom Scholem: Kabbalah and Counter-History*. Cambridge, Ma.: Harvard University Press, 1979.

Bilik, Dorothy S. *Immigrant Survivors: Post-Holocaust Consciousness in Recent Jewish Fiction*. Middleton, Conn.: Wesleyan University Press, 1981.

Bloch, Joshua. *On the Apocalyptic in Judaism*. Jewish Quarterly Review Monograph Series, #2. Philadelphia: Dropsie College for Hebrew and Cognate Learning, 1952.

Bloom, Harold. *Figures of Capable Imagination*. New York: The Seabury Press, 1976.

––––––. Review of *Spectral Emanations* by John Hollander. *New Republic* 179 (9 September 1978), 42–43.

––––––. "The White Light of Trope: An Essay on John Hollander's 'Spectral Emanations.'" *Kenyon Review* NS 1 (Winter 1979), 95–113.

Brumm, Ursula. "Thoughts on History and the Novel." *Comparative Literature Studies* 6 (1969), 317–330.

Cohen, Arthur A. *The Myth of the Judeo-Christian Tradition*. New York: Harper and Row, 1970.

Collins, John J. *The Apocalyptic Vision of the Book of Daniel*. Harvard Semitic Monographs #16. Missoula, Montana: Scholars Press for Harvard Semitic Museum, 1977.

The Encyclopedia Judaica. 16 vols. Jerusalem: Keter Publishing House, 1972.

Ezrahi, Sidra DeKoven. *By Words Alone: The Holocaust in Literature*. Chicago: The University of Chicago Press, 1980.

Feuchtwanger, Leon. *The House of Desdemona; or, The Laurels and Limitations of Historical Fiction*. Translated by Harold A. Basilius. Detroit: Wayne State University Press, 1963.

Frost, Stanley Brice. "Apocalyptic and History." In *The Bible in Modern*

Scholarship. Papers read at the 100th Meeting of the Society of Biblical Literature. 28–30 December 1964. Nashville, Tenn.: Abingdon Press, 1965, 98–113.

———. *Old Testament Apocalyptic: Its Origins and Growth.* London: Epworth Press, 1952.

Gardner, Thomas. "American Poetry of the 1970s: A Preface." *Contemporary Literature* 23: 4 (1982), 407–409.

Greenstone, Julius H. *The Messiah Idea in Jewish History.* Philadelphia: The Jewish Publication Society of America, 1906.

Gross, Harvey. *Contrived Corriders.* Ann Arbor: University of Michigan Press, 1971.

Henderson, Harry B. *Versions of the Past: The Historical Imagination in American Fiction.* New York: Oxford University Press, 1974.

Hollander, John. *The Figure of Echo: A Mode of Allusion in Milton and After.* Berkeley: University of California Press, 1981.

———. *Rhyme's Reason: A Guide to English Verse.* New Haven: Yale University Press, 1981.

Jackson, Richard. "John Hollander, 1978: Candle in the Pitcher." In *Acts of Mind: Conversations with Contemporary Poets.* Tuscaloosa: University of Alabama Press, 1983, 196–205.

Jellinek, Adolph. *Philosophie und Kabbala.* Leipzig: Heinrich Hunger, 1854.

The Jewish Encyclopedia. 12 vols. New York: Funk and Wagnalls, 1901.

Kermode, Frank. "An Approach through History." In *Towards a Poetics of Fiction.* Edited by Mark Spilka. Bloomington: Indiana University Press, 1977, 23–30.

———. *The Sense of an Ending: Studies in the Theory of Fiction.* New York: Oxford University Press, 1967.

Kostelanetz, Richard. *The Old Poetries and the New.* Ann Arbor: University of Michigan Press, 1981.

Lange, Victor. "Fact in Fiction." *Comparative Literature Studies* 6 (1969), 253–261.

Langer, Lawrence. *The Holocaust and Literary Imagination.* New Haven: Yale University Press, 1975.

Lawrence, D. H. *Apocalypse and the Writings on Revelation.* Edited by Mara Kalnes. Cambridge: Cambridge University Press, 1980.

Lewis, R. W. B. "Days of Wrath and Laughter." In his *Trials of the Word: Essays in American Literature and the Humanistic Tradition.* New Haven: Yale University Press, 1965, 184–235.

Lukacs, Georg. *The Historical Novel.* Translated by Hannah and Stanley Mitchell. New York: Humanities Press, 1965.

May, John R. *Toward a New Earth: Apocalypse in the American Novel.* Notre Dame: University of Notre Dame Press, 1972.

Meisl, Josef. "Jewish Historical Writing." In *The Jew: Essays from Martin Buber's Journal "Der Jude," 1916-1928.* Edited by Arthur A. Cohen. Translated by Joachim Neuroschel. University, Ala.: University of Alabama Press, 1980, 198–211.

Milfull, John. "The Messiah and the Direction of History: Walter Benjamin, Isaac Bashevis Singer, and Franz Kafka." In *Festschrift for E. W. Herd.* Otago German Studies, vol. I. Edited by August Obermayer. Dunedin, New Zealand: Department of German, University of Otago, 1980, 180–187.

Morris, Leon. *Apocalyptic.* Grand Rapids, Mich.: William Eerdmans Publishing Company, 1972.

Neuman, Abraham A. "Romance and Realism in Jewish History." In *Essays in Honor of Solomon B. Freehof.* Edited by Walter Jacob, Frederick C. Schwartz, and Vigdor W. Kavala. Pittsburg, Pa.: Rudolph Shalom Congregation, 1964, 246–256.

North, Christopher R. *The Old Testament Interpretation of History.* London: The Epworth Press, 1946.

Patai, Raphael. *The Hebrew Goddess.* Phaladelphia: KTAV Publishing House, Inc., 1967.

Perloff, Marjorie. "From Image to Action: The Return of Story." *Contemporary Literature* 23: 4 (1982), 411–427.

Rawidowicz, Simon. "On Interpretation." In *Studies in Jewish Thought.* Edited by Nahum N. Glatzer. Philadelphia: Jewish Publication Society of America, 1974, 45–47.

Renault, Mary. "History in Fiction." *Times Literary Supplement,* 23 March 1973, pp. 314–316.

Rosenfeld, Alvin H. "Arthur A. Cohen's Messiah." *Midstream,* August–September 1973, 72–75.

———. *A Double Dying: Reflections on Holocaust Literature.* Bloomington: Indiana University Press, 1980.

——— and Irving Greenberg, eds. *Confronting the Holocaust: The Impact of Elie Wiesel.* Bloomington: Indiana University Press, 1978.

Roskies, David G. *Against the Apocalypse: Responses to Catastrophe in Modern Jewish Culture.* Cambridge, Ma.: Harvard University Press, 1984.

Rothenberg, Jerome. "New Models, New Visions: Some Notes Toward a Poetics of Performance." In *Performance in Postmodern Culture.* Edited by Michel Benamou and Charles Caramello. Center for Twentieth-Century Studies, University of Wisconsin-Milwaukee. Madison: Coda Press, 1977, 11–17.

————. *Pre-Faces and Other Writings*. New York: A New Directions Book, 1981.

———— and Diane, eds. *Symposium of the Whole: A Range of Discourse Toward an Ethopoetics*. Berkeley: University of California Press, 1983.

Russell, D. S. *The Method and Message of Jewish Apocalyptic: 200 BC–AD 100*. London: SCM Press, Ltd., 1964.

Sarachek, Joseph. *The Doctrine of the Messiah in Medieval Jewish Literature*. New York: Jewish Theological Seminary of America, 1932.

Sayre, Henry M. "David Antin and the Oral Poetics Movement." *Contemporary Literature* 23: 4 (1982), 428–450.

Scholem, Gershom. *Major Trends in Jewish Mysticism*. New York: Schocken Books, 1961.

————. *Messianic Idea in Judaism and Other Essays on Jewish Spirituality*. New York: Schocken Books, 1971.

————. *On the Kabbalah and its Symbolism*. Translated by Ralph Manheim. New York: Schocken Books, 1965.

————. *Sabbatai Sevi: The Mystical Messiah, 1626–1676*. Bollingen Series XCIII. Princeton, N.J.: Princeton University Press, 1973.

Schwarzschild, Steven S. "The Personal Messiah." In *Arguments and Doctrines: A Reader of Jewish Thinking in the Aftermath of the Holocaust*. Edited by Arthur A. Cohen. New York: Harper and Row, Publishers, 1970, 519–537.

Sharot, Stephen. *Messianism, Mysticism, and Magic: A Sociological Analysis of Jewish Religious Movements*. Chapel Hill: University of North Carolina Press, 1982.

Silver, Abba Hillel. *A History of Messianic Speculation in Israel: From the First through the Seventeenth Centuries*. New York: The Macmillan Company, 1927.

Turner, Joseph W. "The Kinds of Historical Fiction: An Essay in Definition and Methodology." *Genre* 12 (Fall 1979), 333–355.

Wakosi, Diane. *Toward a New Poetry*. Ann Arbor: University of Michigan Press, 1980.

Weinstein, Mark. "The Creative Imagination in Fiction and History." *Genre* 9 (Fall 1976), 263–277.

White, Hayden. "The Fictions of Factual Representation." In *The Literature of Fact: Selected Papers from the English Institute*. Edited by Angus Fletcher. New York: Columbia University, 1976, 21–44.

————. "The Historical Text as Literary Artifact." In *The Writing of History: Literary Form and Historical Understanding*. Edited by Robert H. Canary and Henry Kozicki. Madison: University of Wisconsin Press, 1978, 41–62.

————."The Structure of Historical Narrative." *Clio* 1: iii (1972), 5–20.

Index

Abulafia, Abraham, 12, 27, 44–48,
61, 100–101; *Haye Olam Ha-Ba*,
29, 44; as Messiah, 12, 27, 55;
The Path of the Names, 29–30; as
Raziel, 29, 47, 50; *Sepher Ha-Ot*,
29; *Sha'erei Zedek*, 47, 97; as
Zechariah, 29
Abulafianism, 12, 27–31, 67–68, 83,
106–107; and apocalyptic, 29;
Lettrism, compared to, 30; and
linguistic theory, 27–31, 83, 94,
97, 99–108; and meditation, 28,
30, 47, 97; and prophecy, 27;
and *sephiroth*, 27; Seventy-Two
Letter Name or seventy-two
names of God, 28. *See also*
Gematria, Lettrism, Isidore Isou,
Notarikon, and *Zeruf*
Adam Kadmon. See Lurianism; cosmo-
gonic myth of
Akiba, Rabbi, 22, 40
Angelology. *See* Apocalyptic: angelology
Apocalyptic, 22; angelology. 15, 19,
23, 26–27, 58–60; and
catastrophe, 16; and cosmology,

16, 17; and determinism, 23; and
dualism, 18, 23; and eschatology,
16, 17; and exile, 14–16;
historiography in, 15, 18–19,
24–25, 26, 37, 51–52, 55,
74–81, 93; history of, 16, 23–36;
and linguistic theory, 16; literary
style of, 19, 23–24; and myth,
17, 19; and numerology, 24;
pessimistic optimism of, 18; prophecy, contrast to, 18–19, 39;
pseudonyms in, 19, 23; rejection
of, 12–14; secular literature, relationship to, 19–20; symbolism in,
19, 23, 24–25, 26; and theodicy,
18; and theology, 16; visions in,
15, 19, 23, 26
Apocalyptic Messianism. *See* Messianism: apocalyptic
Ari, The. *See* Luria, Isaac
Ashkenazim, 2, 12
Autobiography: and exile/return,
75–80

Bar Kochba, Simon, 22, 40

133